Henry Hartzler

Moody in Chicago

The World's Fair gospel campaign

Henry Hartzler

Moody in Chicago
The World's Fair gospel campaign

ISBN/EAN: 9783337281731

Printed in Europe, USA, Canada, Australia, Japan

Cover: Foto ©Thomas Meinert / pixelio.de

More available books at **www.hansebooks.com**

MOODY IN CHICAGO

OR

THE WORLD'S FAIR GOSPEL CAMPAIGN

AN ACCOUNT OF

SIX MONTHS' EVANGELISTIC WORK IN
THE CITY OF CHICAGO AND VICINITY
DURING THE TIME OF THE WORLD'S
COLUMBIAN EXPOSITION, CON-
DUCTED BY DWIGHT L.
MOODY AND HIS
ASSOCIATES

BY THE

REV. H. B. HARTZLER

FLEMING H. REVELL COMPANY

NEW YORK   CHICAGO   TORONTO

Publishers of Evangelical Literature

A PREFATORY WORD

SINCE the spring and summer of America's memorable Columbian Year all the world has heard about Chicago, the World's Fair, and the evangelistic movement associated with both, under command of Dwight L. Moody. Fragments of the history of the eventful six months have gone abroad on the wings of the press and by the mouths of the visitors, whithersoever they returned to their homes, even to the ends of the earth. Those who came and saw and heard for themselves could at best see and know only in part, for the colossal whole was too great for comprehension during the exciting days of a brief visit. Those who did not come had their curiosity still more deeply stirred by what they heard from others and read in the papers. For both classes alike it was desirable to secure reliable and sufficient published accounts for themselves and others. This want has been well met, so far as the city and the World's Fair are concerned, with a variety of publications, pictorial and descriptive.

But nothing has yet been written to answer the numerous and multiplying requests for information concerning the extraordinary religious, spiritual movement which ran parallel with the Fair, and which has accomplished more valuable and lasting results for Chicago and the world than the beautiful "White City," with all its surpassing splendor and glory. The demand for some intelligible account of that movement is a reasonable one. There are many thousands of grateful men and women who have come in contact with it and received spiritual benefit thereby; there are others who participated in it to some extent; and still other thousands who know of it only from hearsay and from fragmentary notices in the papers. To all of these a brief history of the work would be welcome and useful. It is to meet this demand, in response to special requests, and with the hope of doing good by still further extending the influence of the gospel work herein described, that this brief record has been prepared.

It is due to the writer, in presenting this volume to the public, to state that its preparation was undertaken, by special request, with the intention of writing, at first hand, a systematic, orderly account of the six months' work of the campaign, from his own point of view, and mainly from his own observation and experience. But on second thought it has seemed more desirable to let the reader have the benefit of the observations and conclusions of other capable participants and witnesses also, which were reported when the fresh glow of the movement was upon their hearts, even though the same ground be traversed more than once by so doing.

It is due to the several writers and speakers whose material has been thus freely appropriated from various periodicals to say that the writer has ventured to take the liberty to make such corrections, changes, or additions as have seemed to him desirable in adapting it to his purpose, and would herewith gratefully acknowledge his obligations to the respected friends for the valuable help thus obtained.

Still another prefatory word should be said. The reader must not expect to find in these pages a complete account of the manifold details of the evangelistic campaign. Two thousand pages would not suffice to contain such an account. It is believed that this book, as it is, will serve a better purpose than would one drawn up on a larger scale and with a wider compass. In this confidence, with the hope that it may bear the echoes and the lessons of the great movement into the hearts of multitudes, and multiply to them the blessings already made manifest therein, this little volume is trustfully committed to the Hand that guides all things to their destined end.

H. B. HARTZLER.

EAST NORTHFIELD, MASS.

CONTENTS

WORLD'S FAIR CAMPAIGN

CHAPTER I.

THE CITY AND THE EVANGELIST.

FIFTY years ago an English writer characterized the nineteenth century as "the age of great cities." It was true then; it is most startlingly true now. Since that writer's day the comparative growth of city population has been rapid beyond all precedent in the history of the world. Year by year the tributary streams of life pouring into the great city centers have been growing deeper, fuller, stronger, draining away the rural population in larger proportion than ever before. It is one of the striking and significant phenomena of our time.

It has always been true that the controlling agencies and influences of civilization have been centered and massed in the cities. It is more tremendously true to-day than ever before. The city, in the language of Dr. Josiah Strong, is "the Gibraltar of civilization." It is "the strategic point" for all movements upon society, for weal or for woe. "It is the mighty heart of the body politic, which sends its streams of life pulsating to the very finger-tips of the whole land; and when the blood becomes poisoned, it poisons every fiber of the whole body." In the cities are massed and intrenched in greatest strength the giant enemies that threaten our civilization.   These enemies more than keep pace with the growth of the cities, and the peril and the menace increase year by year. Among the great perils confronting us everywhere, but concentrated in the cities, and therefore greatly enhanced there, Dr. Strong specifies especially "wealth, its worship and its congestion, anarchism and lawlessness, intemperance and the liquor power, immigration and a superstitious Christianity."   In face of these facts, conditions, and perils the special need and supreme importance of city evangelization need no argument.

The present is not only the age of great cities, it is also the age of Christian evangelism.   Never has the open field of the world been so extensively and systematically invaded by evangelistic agencies as now.   Evangelistic leaders, lay and clerical, have become a vast army.   There is hardly a city or large town in our land, or in Christendom, that has not experienced the sensation of concentrated and continuous evangelistic effort, and hardly a church, or other Christian agency, that has not felt the stimulus and reaped more or less beneficial results therefrom.

The ways and means of evangelistic effort have been as various as the evangelists and the conditions under which they have prosecuted their labors.   But as the result of years of such labors by hundreds of evangelists, especially in the cities, they have come to an almost uniform general course of procedure wherever an extensive work has been undertaken.   The aim has been, first of all, to secure the coöperation of the churches, to revive their own piety and zeal, and, if practicable, unite and prepare their forces for an organized movement upon the unsaved masses.   After every such campaign the evangelistic leader would depart to other fields, leaving to the revived churches the care of the converts, and any further prosecution of the work, according to their own pleasure. In the city of Chicago, under the peculiar and extraordinary conditions of the World's Fair season, the usual means and methods would not apply. A new line of action had to be taken, for which the history of evangelism furnished no precedent, unless it was in the pentecostal meeting in Jerusalem.

The first evangelistic movement of the present dispensation, under immediate divine direction, was started in a great cosmopolitan city center, the capital of the Jewish nation. It was an occasion when vast multitudes of visitors, from all parts of the earth, had overflowed the city and doubled its population. It was a time of special interest and excitement, and of unusual activity, when the people had eyes and ears for anything that was to be seen and heard. The time, the place, the conditions, all were favorable to the inauguration of the new movement.

After the first blow had been struck in that city center, and the saving impression had been made upon the great multitude, the visiting thousands from other lands and cities returned with the new story and the new sensation to their own homes. Then followed an outward movement, directed by the enthroned Christ himself, for the evangelization of the world. In widening circles, rolling out from the city center, the new force invaded the expectant nations. Beginning in one great city, it followed a line of movement that struck through the hearts of other great cities, from Jerusalem to Rome. The flame, bursting out suddenly in the Jewish metropolis, after the pre-pentecostal pause, kindled successively the cities of Antioch, Ephesus, Athens, Corinth, and Rome. There were the central fires lighted and kept burning for the illumination of the nations.

The marvelous story of that first Christian evangelization movement is preserved for us in the Acts of the
Apostles, that we may see and know, once for all, the
divine thought and method working out before our eyes.
In grand outline it is the chart along whose clearly traced
lines the organized movements of Christian world-conquest
are to be conducted to the end of the age. In that genesis
of the new dispensation lie the germs and roots of all its
development, the principles of its life and action, even to
the consummation foreseen and foretold by the guiding
Spirit of God. There is an unerring, superintending
Providence over all. As there were in the first days, so
there are in these latter days, prepared places, opportune
times, favoring conditions, divine intimations and tokens,
which it needs only the ready, open-eyed, Spirit-guided
disciple to see and to take advantage of, in order to realize
the same results. God must have his own way still, and
the secret of power lies in human coöperation with him,
that his will may be done.

CHAPTER II.

ALL men everywhere need salvation, and salvation in the gospel is offered to all. The city needs it; the country needs it. There is no difference. That there are more people in the city than in the country makes no difference as to the need of the individual. But the aggregation of individuals in the cities creates perils on the one hand, and offers opportunities on the other, which call for evangelistic efforts on a larger scale, of a more comprehensive character, not alone for the salvation of the individual sinner and the edification of the individual believer, but also for the salvation of society itself. An invasion of a wicked city by bold, aggressive, evangelistic forces, flashing the uncompromising truth of God into the faces of the selfish, preoccupied multitudes, piercing the darkness with its startling light of eternity, may save it from corruption and destruction by the very shock of the new sensation. This awakening, alarming invasion is the crying need of the cities in these fearfully intense days, when selfishness, greed, avarice, oppression, lust, vice, and crime are driving on with electric power and speed, regardless and almost oblivious of the ordinary, accustomed Sabbath-day religious services of the churches. The heedless city must be compelled to listen, by assailing its ears from unaccustomed quarters and with new voices. It is a great thing just to secure such an arrest of thought; to create a

15

diversion in the direction of spiritual and eternal things; to break the lines and confuse the marching step of the great multitudes of the cities in the awful unanimity of their mad rush for self-gratification, whose issue is self-destruction. This can be accomplished only by extraordinary efforts, in extraordinary ways, with extraordinary power.

Now, if this be true of cities under ordinary, every-day conditions, when the currents of life and activity are flowing on in their accustomed channels, much more is the need of extraordinary religious effort emphasized when those currents are swelled by the inflow of hundreds of thousands of souls, till they rush on with a tumultuous violence threatening an overflow, and drowning the accustomed voices of sermon and song in their constant roar, as was the case with Chicago during the time of the World's Fair. It is well known that even under ordinary circumstances this greatest, richest, strongest, most enterprising city of the West constitutes one of the most extensive, peculiar, and difficult fields for evangelistic work. Its population of more than 1,400,000 souls embraces almost all nationalities of the earth, and in many cases the worst types of humanity out of those nationalities. A strong irreligious and antireligious foreign and native element is always present and potent. Multitudes there are "who never had any religion, and who don't want any," and who will not suffer anybody else to have any, if they can help it.

An observing writer, considering Chicago as a field for evangelistic work, says: "The city is full of people who once had church relations, but since coming here have neglected to join a local society; and among the masses there are thousands who have broken their connections with religious organizations on leaving Europe and never renewed them. Then, too, the location of the city and its character as a commercial center bring in an innumerable host of homeless men who are under little or no moral restraint, and give pecuniary support to the most degraded and degrading elements of the community, as well as themselves, constituting a powerful factor toward evil. That infidelity is wide-spread and ignorance dominant is well known. Prejudice on the part of the masses against the church is a natural outcome of the industrial disturbances of the day and the attendant oppression of the poor. The vast population of the city and the barriers of class and race and tongue enhance the difficulty of evangelistic work, while the need of such effort is nowhere more urgent."

During the time of the World's Fair, as a matter of course, the need and the difficulty of evangelistic effort were still further increased, not only by the constant ebb and flow of the great tides of respectable humanity, but especially by the influx of the worst elements, reinforcing the idle, the vicious, and the criminal classes of the population. Add to this the intensified activities in every sphere of life and labor, and the overwhelming, bewildering attractions, distractions, and excitement of the Fair and its concomitants, and it goes without saying that the religious outlook for Chicago was anything but promising. The most experienced and spiritual of the pastors and people of the city looked forward to it with altogether reasonable misgivings and apprehensions. "It was a question," said one of the chief pastors, "what was to become of us during the six months. We knew at best it would be a time of great excitement, and what should become of the spiritual life of the churches we knew not." They did know that even under ordinary circumstances it had been found almost impossible to maintain the full life and activity of the churches and the various Christian agencies during the summer season. How much less could they hope even to hold their own, under the extraordinary circumstances of the season, to say nothing of making spiritual conquests and gains of the overflowing multitudes from abroad. Chicago people, it was said, would have no time to go to religious meetings, with all their extra work, business and pleasures, entertainment of visitors, sight-seeing, and other demands upon their time and attention incident to the season. And as for the people who would visit Chicago, it was concluded that of course they came to see and study the great exposition, and certainly not to attend religious meetings. Indeed, the crowds of pleasure-seekers would be only too glad to get out of sight and hearing of preachers and preaching for a time.

It is to be remembered that it was in full view of all these forbidding and discouraging facts and considerations, against the judgment of wise and good men, and without any warrant of precedent, that Mr. D. L. Moody moved forward to do what an eminent minister characterized as "the boldest and most daring thing that had been undertaken in connection with the Columbian Exposition." It was purely a work of faith, undertaken with the conviction that it was of God and for God. Human misgivings and fears were not admitted into the council. If God wanted the thing done, he could get it done. He wanted it done. It was done. And so it has come to pass that the red threads of the great gospel campaign conducted by Mr. Moody have been interwoven with the history of Chicago, the World's Fair, and the Columbian Year.

CHAPTER III.

MR. MOODY arrived in Chicago in the month of May, 1893, with his mind fully made up to inaugurate a series of meetings for the preaching of the gospel, which were to run parallel with the proposed six months' term of the World's Fair. He had but lately returned from one of the most extensive evangelistic campaigns of his life, of fourteen months' duration, in England, Scotland, Ireland, and the Orient. So far as there was any plan of the proposed movement in Chicago, it was laid up in the secret of his own mind. He was not committed to any published program. As always in his work, he placed himself in line with the will of God, ready to do the next thing, whatever that might be.

The thought and purpose of attempting such an unheard-of enterprise had been formed in Mr. Moody's mind long before the World's Fair itself had become a materialized fact. He carried the matter on his heart during his long evangelistic tours in Europe and his trip to the Holy Land. It was then that he enlisted the help of representative men of Christian Europe for the prosecution of the prospective work. The only thing concerning the proposed gospel campaign which was positively settled in his mind was the conviction that it was the will of God that it should be inaugurated. He could well foresee that the material glory of the Fair would attract millions of people, "out of every nation under heaven," and his heart yearned and burned with desire to make it an opportunity for the kingdom of God, by having the gospel preached with a world-wide reach of influence and effect. It was enough for him to see the finger of God, "in the signs of the times," pointing that way, and he hesitated not a moment to confer with flesh and blood. In its conception, beginning, and progress it was therefore purely a work of faith and a labor of love. When the time for the actual work had come, Mr. Moody entered upon it not only with conviction of the divine call, and desire and zeal for the salvation of men, but also as a man under seal of the most solemn vow, as we learn from the following reference to his memorable experience on his homeward voyage from Europe, given in a public address:

"Just as I was preparing to leave London the last time I was there, I called upon a celebrated physician, who told me that my heart was weakening, and that I had to let up on my work, that I had to be more careful of myself; and I was going home with the thought that I would not work quite so hard. I was on the steamer *Spree*, and when the announcement came that the vessel was sinking, and we were there forty-eight hours in a helpless condition, no one on earth knows what I passed through during those hours, as I thought that my work was finished, and that I would never again have the privilege of preaching the gospel of the Son of God. And on that dark night, the first night of the accident, I made a vow that if God would spare my life and bring me back to America I would come back to Chicago and at this World's Fair preach the gospel with all the power that he would give me; and God has enabled me to keep that vow during the past five months. It seems as if I went to the very gates of heaven during those forty-eight hours on

the sinking ship, and God permitted me to come back and
preach Christ a little longer."

It is to be noted also that in England, Scotland, and
Ireland, the year before, Mr. Moody made public reference
to the work he proposed to carry on in Chicago, and asked
that God's children should remember the undertaking in
prayer. Indeed, he seemed more concerned that it should
have the assurance and support of united prayer than
anything else. After his return to America he laid the
matter entreatingly and earnestly on the hearts of Christian people, seeking a union of fervent prayer in behalf of
the work. At Northfield and Mount Hermon he gathered
the students and teachers of his schools about him, at six
o'clock in the morning, to seek the anointing of the Holy
Spirit, and to pray for the work to come. "If you think
anything of me," said he, with choking voice and tear-
filled eyes, "if you have any regard for me, if you love
me, pray for me that God may anoint me for the work in
Chicago. I want to be filled with the Spirit, that I may
preach the gospel as I never preached it before. We
want to see the salvation of God as we have never seen it
before." During the entire campaign there was unusual
stress laid on prayer as the indispensable condition of
success. It was a campaign of prayer as much as a campaign of preaching and of song. In conferences, churches,
Christian societies, at family altars, and in the closet, the
evangelists and their work were made the subject of special prayer. By some means an almost world-wide interest and sympathy in the movement were created, with a
wonderful passion and concord of prayer in its behalf, as
if God himself had laid the burden upon thousands of
hearts, afar and near. The fact was accepted as God's
gracious token and pledge of favor and blessing.

Not only did the leaders in the campaign pray without

ceasing, but they labored to bring the people into the same spirit. Prayer was the prominent exercise in the meetings. Special seasons of prayer were also observed. The first day of the month of August was marked by a meeting for humiliation and prayer, which was held in the Empire Theater, and which Mr. Moody characterized as one of the best he ever attended. The afternoon of the 1st of September was signalized in the same way, by a meeting in the Chicago Avenue Church, to which the ministers of the city and all praying people were invited. A large congregation assembled, and for one hour waited before the Lord in prayer, uniting in spirit with petitions uttered by English, Scotch, American, Swedish, and German voices. It was as though the suppliants said: "Here we raise our Ebenezer. Hither by thy help, O Lord, we have come. And by thy good pleasure we hope to have a yet more prosperous month in work for thee. We claim thy promised presence, power, and grace. We rest in thee."

CHAPTER IV.

THE CAMPAIGN COMMENCED.

AT the corner of La Salle and Chicago Avenues stands the well-known Chicago Avenue Church, better known as "Moody's Church," which owes its existence to the labors of the evangelist. It is a large, substantial brick building, with a seating capacity of twenty-two hundred in the auditorium, and almost equal space in the lecture-room and class-rooms on the first floor. In the same block, and close to the church, are the buildings of the Chicago Bible Institute, of which Mr. Moody is the founder and president. It was according to the fitness of things that the opening meeting of the World's Fair Evangelistic Campaign should take place in the historic church established by its projector and leader, especially since the entire work was to be inseparably connected with the church and the Bible Institute. It was on the first Sunday in May, a bright, beautiful, auspicious morning. The people came early, and soon the church presented the familiar scene of stairways and aisles, gallery and floor, packed with a solid mass of eager, earnest listeners and worshipers, with the burly form of Mr. Moody standing well to the front, surveying the throng, and directing all the preliminaries of the service, and his not less stalwart co-partner, Mr. Sankey, leading the songs.

On the platform, at this first meeting, were seated such well-known helpers as Major D. W. Whittle, Rev. R. A.

Torrey, superintendent of the Bible Institute, Rev. T. B. Hyde, pastor of the church, and an array of singers, including such leaders as Professor D. B. Towner, H. H. McGranahan, and Mrs. F. T. Pierson, besides Mr. Sankey.

The introductory sermon was preached by Mr. Moody. To the surprise of many he chose for his subject "The Elder Brother," in the story of the prodigal son. It was not, perhaps, obvious at first why he should have taken such a theme for such an occasion; but he is not often found acting without a motive, and it soon became evident that his desire was to disarm and condemn the prejudices which often excite opposition to the work of reclaiming the lost.

"There are quite a number of such men," he said, "right here in this city to-day; they are very religious in outward observance, but they do not know how to sympathize with a prodigal, nor help those who try to lift him up." In his own inimitable way, the preacher went on to demonstrate that there is not one of the Beatitudes the elder brother had not violated, thus placing himself quite outside the sphere of the Spirit of Christ. In short, he was the meanest man in history. Externally he was all right, internally he was all wrong, and yet he resembles many Christians to-day, nearer than they suppose. His father sought that *both* his sons should be with him; and that is just what God the Father wants; he has room for us all. But many people want the benefit of religion themselves while they grudge it to their neighbors, and try to secure heaven without being identified with the Father "through our Lord Jesus Christ." If they cannot get it on their own terms, they "will not go in." "Arise and claim thy sonship, and hear thy Heavenly Father say, 'All that I have is thine.'"

In the afternoon the church was again filled with an

expectant multitude. Mr. Moody again was the speaker. At this meeting he struck a different note. The hearts of many were, perhaps not unnaturally, turned in the direction of "prayer," but the preacher went further than that, and spoke upon "praise"—praise in anticipation of blessing to come during the next weeks. He would have every Christian heart in an attitude of expectancy, warm with gratitude, and strong in the confidence of faith. It was fitting that such a service should consist largely of praise expressed in song. Some of the old familiar hymns rolled forth from two or three thousand voices, and the singers above named, with the Oberlin Quartet, rendered some of the most delightful of the hymns of the heart.

A third meeting of the Sunday was held in the same church in the evening. Mr. Moody's sermon was addressed especially to the unsaved. He pressed upon them the pleading appeal and the sweet promise of Isaiah lv. 7.

At the same hour the gospel was preached and sung in Dr. Goodwin's Congregational Church, by Major Whittle and Mr. Sankey, and in La Salle Avenue Baptist Church, by Rev. R. A. Torrey, with Professor Towner and Mrs. Pierson. Services were also conducted by numerous students from the Bible Institute in different districts. These were, of course, all in affiliation with Mr. Moody's campaign, but it was also very gratifying to learn that *the churches generally* throughout the city were exceptionally well attended—an indication that among the World's Fair visitors there were many whose delight was in the things of God.

In the meetings of the opening Sunday could be plainly discerned the spirit and purpose of the movement of which they were the beginning. During the week following, without special tokens of interest or encouragement, a series of praise services were held in the Chicago Avenue

Church, as though the difficult and daring undertaking had already been accomplished. It is probable that even amidst circumstances which to others seemed forbidding and discouraging, Mr. Moody heard "the sound of a going," for he never looked back, nor wavered in the calm confidence and resolute will with which he had come up to the work.

The second Sunday Mr. Moody again preached, morning and evening, in the Chicago Avenue Church, and conducted a praise and prayer service in the afternoon. During the week the meetings were multiplied, the speakers being, besides Mr. Moody, the venerable Scotch missionary apostle, Dr. John G. Paton, Rev. Charles Inwood, and Rev. Hubert Brooke. In addition to the evangelistic evening meetings, two daily Bible lectures were delivered at the Bible Institute by Dr. W. G. Moorehead and the two speakers last named. Although a part of the regular daily program of the Bible Institute, these lectures contributed no small part toward the sum total of impulse and power by which the work of evangelism was carried forward, for in the Bible Institute were assembled the hundreds of enlisted Christian workers and evangelistic leaders, as well as a host of Christian visitors from this and other lands, who needed the strong meat of the Word there set before them.

Mr. George E. Morgan, of the London *Christian*, a participant in the earlier part of the work, says that during the first two weeks of his labors Mr. Moody was occupied in more fully maturing and developing his plans for the wide-spread evangelization of Chicago, as well as for the salvation and edification of the strangers within her gates. The need for such effort was most painfully apparent, not only to the stranger from abroad, but also to those residents who were concerned for the spiritual welfare of

the city. "There is," says Mr. Morgan, "a general slack-
ness as to moral and religious matters with which even
London cannot compare. The outward observance of the
Lord's Day is reduced to a minimum; stores and shops
are open; work and traffic on the streets and railways
going on; everybody doing what he will in this respect,
without let or hindrance. The theaters have performances on Sunday afternoons and evenings; and the seven
thousand saloons with which the city is cursed are practically open, the 'Sunday closing' being confined to the
drawing down of a window-blind, while the unfastened
doors invite all comers. In short, the 'Continental' Sunday prevails in all its worst features."

CHAPTER V.

LIGHT IN A DARK PLACE.

FOR many years Mr. Moody had a particular section of the city laid upon his heart, and to this his energies were being especially directed during the first weeks of his campaign. It is the section embracing the Haymarket, Standard, and Empire theaters, of West Madison and Halstead Streets, with their saloons, brothels, gambling-hells, murderers' dens, and all kinds of vile resorts. Having first secured a four-storied building, he opened the ground floor as a mission hall, the upper rooms being devoted to sleeping and living accommodation for thirty of his students, whom he for the time being quartered there. Situate on a busy, main thoroughfare, West Madison Street, near the Haymarket and the Empire theaters, it could hardly help attracting some of the throngs of passers-by. At 2 P.M. each day the hall was opened for singing and conversation, while the neighborhood was visited from house to house by the rest of the workers in view of the evening's work. A gospel meeting, preceded by half an hour's singing, was held from seven to eight, followed by an hour for private conversation with inquirers. At 10 P.M. a second meeting of an hour's duration was held by another relay of workers, who also occupied an hour till midnight in dealing with the anxious and unsaved. By this means it was hoped to reach those whose only evening resort is the saloon bar, and the result soon justified the hope and the effort. The building is now known as Institute Hall, and is a permanent part of the evangelizing agencies of the Chicago Bible Institute.

An observer well acquainted with Chicago life and work, writing about the band of workers connected with Institute Hall, says: "One cannot help admiring the earnestness and courage of these young men and women, who go about their work with an enthusiasm which ought to be, if it is not, contagious among Christians in Chicago. One day, as we were returning by way of Madison Street, we were surprised to see a band of these students with their organ on the sidewalk in front of Institute Hall, one of the headquarters of their work, singing to the immense crowds coming and going along this crowded thoroughfare on Saturday evening, the liveliest of the week. After a service of song on the sidewalk they held their regular evening meeting in their audience-room, which is a store opening on to the street, appropriately arranged with a raised platform at the front of the hall for speakers, singers, and the organ, mottoes or texts upon the walls, with electric fans for ventilation, well lighted and seated, and seemingly as well managed, while the location could not be better, it being on one of the most traveled streets of a crowded quarter of our city."

Another writer thus refers to the same work: "The hall is open every evening at ten o'clock for a rescue service. Good singing and an attractive room draw in the tired and aimless wanderers of the street. They are a pitiable lot of men, some too drunk to control themselves, almost all of them under the power of the drink habit, and, with few exceptions, reduced to destitution and despair. It would be hard to find anywhere in the city a more disappointed and hopeless lot of men, and the very fact of their failure in life and their utter lack of any

bright outlook for the future is the one thing that makes
them approachable. The service is full of spirited music;
Scripture and prayer are alike practical and direct; and
after an earnest presentation of the way of salvation the
truth is enforced by testimony from redeemed men, who
tell how they were saved by the power of Christ from
lives of drunkenness and degradation. Such evidence has
great weight with the hearers, and a great work is being
done among those who have sunk to the lowest level."

CHAPTER VI.

AMONG the serious difficulties encountered by Mr. Moody at the beginning of his work was a want of suitably located places of assembly where the masses of the people could be reached with the gospel. It seemed for a time as if the desirable halls and theaters were all by common consent and "malice aforethought" shut against the evangelistic invaders. The most liberal offers were refused. One instance will indicate what is meant by this. Mr. Moody was anxious to secure the use of the Auditorium, a theater located at Michigan Avenue and Congress Street, for Sunday meetings. The immense sum of $18,500 was offered and refused. Offers for other halls met with no better success. But what then seemed barriers became open doors, for there was a providence in the movement that would not be baffled by man.

One of the most desirable places in the city soon opened its doors to the evangelist. This was the Haymarket Theater, located on West Madison Street, a fine building, perfectly adapted for the desired purpose, with seating capacity for about three thousand persons. In this place morning services were conducted every Sunday until the end of the campaign, Mr. Moody preaching on each occasion, with the exception of two Sundays, when he was absent from the city. Those Haymarket meetings became as well known to the thronging thousands who visited

the World's Fair as the "White City" itself. A more remarkable series of meetings has probably never been held.
It is hardly too much to say that there Mr. Moody and
his glorious singers were brought into contact with the
Christian world. The echoes of those marvelous sermons
and melting songs will go ringing through lands afar and
generations yet to come.

When the engagement was first made for this theater,
it was with the expectation that it would require hard,
persistent work to get Sunday morning congregations.
So Mr. Moody told his workers. "You need not think,"
said he, "that we are going to get an audience down there
for the asking. I know the district well, and I know that
the working-men don't get to bed till 1 or 2 A.M., and they
are not coming to an eleven o'clock meeting without some
pressure. If we want an audience we'll have to go out
and get it, and that means work. We'll have admission
by ticket only, and you'll have to besiege the sidewalk and
the back streets, and get the people out."

Then began the work of stirring up the neighborhood,
and the Bible Institute workers took hold of it with a will.
It proved anything but an easy task. Mr. Morgan tells
of one lady visitor who, with a heart full of love for the
outcast, was met at one house after another with nothing but curses. At last, after a long climb upstairs, she
reached the top of a rickety tenement, only to receive more
vehement oaths than had been cast at her heretofore.
Physically spent and somewhat discouraged, she boldly
tackled her assailant thus: "Now look here, I've had
nothing but curses all this afternoon, so don't you begin.
Please get me a drink of water instead, for I'm done up!"
That "touch of nature" that "makes the whole world kin"
had the desired effect, and resulted in a hospitable reception that was as refreshing as it was unexpected.

Each night of the week preceding the first Haymarket Theater service the Institute Hall, near by, was filled, and the workers had a busy time with inquirers at every meeting. When Sunday morning came it was a joyful surprise to all to see the immense theater packed from floor to ceiling, while the aisles and stage were thronged with those unable to obtain seats. And what of the audience? It was just such a one as was desired. That there was a good sprinkling of the "respectably dressed" element was at once apparent, but in the main it was composed of the class it was intended to reach. The one feature that struck the observer first of all was the great preponderance of men, and a careful computation of row after row in all parts of the house showed that they formed from seventy-five to eighty percent. of the audience, and this in a city where the male element in the churches is represented by a lamentably small proportion. For nearly six months, every Sunday morning, the wonder was repeated —three thousand eager people from all parts of this country and other lands filling every foot of space in the theater, while hundreds were turned away, unable to gain admittance.

Mr. Moody's opening sermon, no less than the succeeding ones, made a profound impression. It was a vivid picture of King Herod and John the Baptist, the murderer and the martyr. At its close, as ever after, he drew the gospel net, always expecting and always realizing immediate results. On this occasion he invited all who were anxious to meet him in the mission hall, a hundred yards away; and there over two hundred men and women thronged in to leave their names and addresses as anxious to receive a book on regeneration which he had promised. It was a really affecting sight. Side by side stood rough men and fashionably dressed ladies, negroes and working-women and gentlemen, all anxiously pressing forward to have their names taken down. Quite a large number were visitors from other States who, passing through the city in pursuit of pleasure or business, were thus arrested by the gospel message, delivered in such terms that the most illiterate could not fail to understand.

CHAPTER VII.

MORE WORK AND WORKERS.

THE week at the Bible Institute and the Chicago Avenue Church was a busy one, the work both enlarging and intensifying. The three missioners, Revs. Hubert Brooke, Charles Inwood, and G. H. C. MacGregor, representing the English Episcopal, the Wesleyan Methodist of Ireland, and the Scotch Presbyterian churches, held meetings three times a day for the deepening of the spiritual life, urging a personal, whole-hearted surrender to the will of God. In introducing the missioners, whom he had invited from beyond the sea, Mr. Moody said: "We cannot lead others nearer to Christ than we are living ourselves, and there is no use working unless we are filled with the Spirit of God. We want to get down on our faces before him, and humble ourselves at his feet. Let him search us and try our thoughts, and see if there be any wicked way in us. This is why I have asked these brethren to come amongst us. They have been greatly used of God in many towns in Canada, and a wave of blessing has come to the churches they have visited. That's just what we want right here in Chicago; and if we get that, then our preaching will be with power, and our work will bear a precious harvest of souls."

The faithful labors of these co-workers were greatly appreciated by Mr. Moody, and richly blessed. To many devout minds they opened new views of truth and Chris-

35

tian privilege and obligation, imparting a decided impulse in the life of faith and service.

The force of workers coöperating with Mr. Moody, in addition to the efficient bands of male and female students and leaders of the Bible Institute, was being constantly augmented by the arrival of invited evangelists and singers, from the first week to the last. Among these arrivals, the fourth week, was one who was to stand side by side with Mr. Moody till the last day of the campaign—Rev. John McNeill, the Scotch evangelist, accompanied by his gospel singer, Mr. J. H. Burke. At a great gathering in the Chicago Avenue Church the new-comer preached his introductory sermon on "David."

After the first four weeks the practicability of a gospel work in Chicago during the World's Fair had been satisfactorily demonstrated. It now only remained to press forward wisely, steadily, resolutely, from point to point, with ever-increasing power, so as to make the utmost of the grand opportunity. It is not possible here to follow the widening circles of the movement through the successive victorious days, weeks, and months. We must content ourselves with a glimpse here and there of parts of the grand whole.

The force of workers which Mr. Moody, as commander-in-chief, gathered around himself was a large one, remarkable alike for variety of gifts, capacity for varied labors, and power for effective service. It may be well to name the principal evangelists, clergymen, and song leaders whose voices were heard in the various meetings of the campaign. At the first meeting Mr. Moody had by his side, on the platform of the Chicago Avenue Church, Major D. W. Whittle, Rev. R. A. Torrey, Ira D. Sankey, D. B. Towner, and H. H. McGranahan. To these were subsequently added the following, among many others whose names cannot here be given: Dr. A. C. Dixon, Brooklyn, N. Y.; Dr. H. M. Wharton, Baltimore, Md.; George C. Needham, East Northfield, Mass.; Dr. J. Wilbur Chapman, Philadelphia; Dr. A. J. Gordon, Boston; Dr. W. G. Moorehead, Xenia, O.; Dr. J. M. Stifler, Crozer Theological Seminary; Dr. C. I. Scofield, Dallas, Tex.; Dr. A. T. Pierson, East Northfield, Mass.; Dr. T. L. Cuyler, Brooklyn; Dr. James H. Brookes, St. Louis, Mo.; Dr. John Hall, New York; Drs. P. S. Henson and J. L. Withrow, Chicago; Dr. A. B. Simpson, New York; Major-General O. O. Howard, U. S. A.; Dr. Joseph Cook, Boston; Rev. B. Fay Mills, Major Cole, Chicago; Rev. R. G. Pearson, Asheville, N. C.; Hon. John G. Woolley, Geo. D. McKay, New York; Rev. Niclaus Boldt, St. Paul, Minn.; Evangelists Ferd. Schiverea, W. Dalgetty, L. P. Rowland, D. W. Potter, Abe Mulke, H. Openshaw, J. H. Elliott, Col. H. H. Hadley, Rev. G. B. Rogers, R. A. Hadden, A. P. Fitt, A. F. Gaylord, C. H. Stevens, and Rev. C. O. Jones, Tennessee; Dr. G. C. Lorimer, Boston; Mr. Stephen Merritt, New York; L. W. Munhall, Philadelphia; Rev. D. Breed, H. L. Hastings, Boston; Merton Smith, Chicago; J. C. Davis and H. I. Higgins, in charge of the gospel carriage; J. W. Deane, President C. A. Blanchard, Wheaton College; Dr. H. Clay Trumbull, of the *Sunday-school Times;* Robert E. Speer, New York; Rev. A. Skoogsbergh.

From beyond the sea were such men as Rev. John McNeill, Dr. John Riddell, Dr. John Robertson, Dr. Hugh Montgomery, Richard Hill, Rev. G. H. C. MacGregor, J. M. Scroggie, W. Robertson, Lord Kinnaird, and John Currie, of Scotland; Henry Varley, Rev. Hubert Brooke, Charles Inglis, Rev. Thomas Spurgeon, Dr. J. Munro Gibson, Lord Bennett, J. E. K. Studd, Mr. Davis, Rev. J. B. Wookey, Rev. Greenwood, of London, England; Dr. John G. Paton, the Missionary Apostle of the New Hebrides; Dr. Adolf

Stoecker, ex-court preacher of Germany; Rabbi Rabinowitz, of Russia; Dr. J. Pindor, of Austria; Dr. Theo. Monod, of Paris; Rev. Charles Inwood, of Ireland; Count
Bernstorff, of Germany.

Among those who labored effectively in the service of
song may be named, in addition to those mentioned in
connection with the opening meeting, George C. Stebbins,
J. H. Burke, F. H. Jacobs, Chess Birch, F. H. Atkinson,
C. Alexander, Mr. Wellicome, Miss Van Valkenburgh, Miss
Henton, the Stebbins and the Towner Male Choirs, and
the Oberlin, Princeton, Kimball, Institute, Torrey, and
Ladies' Institute quartets. The service of song throughout the entire campaign was a magnificent demonstration
of the value, adaptation, and power of this department of
worship and gospel work. Under able leadership a host
of singers could always be mustered on the platform, in
any part of the city.

When it is remembered that Mr. Moody himself is not
a singer, it is the more remarkable that he should have
given so prominent and important a place to the service
of song in all his evangelistic work and in the scheme of
training provided in all his schools. And never was this
service organized and utilized on so large a scale as in this
Chicago campaign. This department of the work excited
the deepest interest and amazement of some of the foreign
visitors. "The service of song," writes one to a foreign
journal, "is an extraordinary feature of these meetings.
The choir and solo songsters are many, and they really
sing for Jesus. Last night hundreds were drawn from
the streets to hear the singing. No wonder they come,
for it is something to hear indeed. The voice of praise
is seldom silent or at rest in this building" (the Bible Institute). In order to secure the service of the best singers
—solo, quartet, and choir—they were often hurried from

one meeting-place to another, so that all the principal
meetings held at the same hours might have the benefit
of their singing.

An immense amount of woman's work entered into the
sum total of the gospel campaign. Quietly, effectively,
pervasively, like a gracious leaven, the consecrated daughters of the King labored on, through the days and nights,
month after month, in perfect accord with the grand movement, and under the one masterful leadership. Among
those who took prominent part may be named Mrs. S. B.
Capron, superintendent of the Ladies' Department of the
Bible Institute; Miss B. B. Tyson, of Washington, D. C.;
Mrs. A. J. Gordon, of Boston; Mrs. E. M. Whittemore, of
New York; Miss Catherine Gurney, of London; and Misses
Emily S. Strong, N. E. McClure, C. E. Waite, Poxon, and
Van Valkenburgh, of the Bible Institute.

Add to these names of preachers, teachers, evangelists,
singers, and others, a great host of unnamed workers
whose hearts God had touched with holy fire and power
—the rank and file of the evangelizing army—some of
whom wrought perhaps more effectively even than their
leaders, and you have before your mind's eye the human
working forces of the campaign. A large part of this
force, as elsewhere noted, consisted of the indispensable
trained workers of the Chicago Bible Institute—a capable,
ready, willing body, always at command of the leader,
whether for speech, song, prayer, or to "serve tables" in
any capacity that the occasion required.

CHAPTER VIII.

ONE very important and difficult part of the management of the campaign, especially at the beginning, was the securing of proper meeting-places as centers of operation. Beginning with the Chicago Avenue Church and the Chapel of the Bible Institute as the central basis of operation, the following places were occupied, some more, some less, according to circumstances: The Haymarket, Empire, Standard, Columbia, Hooley's, Windsor, Tattersall's, and Vaudeville theaters; the Central Music Hall and the Grand Opera House; the Endeavor Hotel Tabernacle, the Epworth Hotel Tabernacle, the Columbian Sunday-school Building, the Hall of Columbus, Turner Hall, Arcade Hall, Willard Hall, Holmes' Hall, Institute Hall, People's Tabernacle, People's Institute, West Side Tabernacle, Pacific Garden Mission, Forepaugh's Circus Tent, the Chicago and the Englewood Y. M. C. A. buildings, and the Pullman Hall, with the following churches in the city and its suburbs: Presbyterian—The First, Second, Third, Fourth, Forty-first Street, Woodlawn, Immanuel, Campbell Park, Covenant, and Englewood; Congregational—The First, Grace, Union Park, Rogers Park, Ewing Street, Plymouth, Warren Avenue, and Lake View; Baptist—Immanuel, Second, Fourth, Bethany, Belden Avenue, Trinity, La Salle Avenue, Langley Avenue, and Englewood; Methodist Episcopal—The First, Western Avenue, Oakwood,

Fulton Street, Trinity, Wesley, South Park Avenue, Blue Island, Auburn Park, Union Park, St. Paul's, Evanston, and Wheaton; two Lutheran churches; St. Paul's Reformed Episcopal; one Bohemian; Noble Street Evangelical; Hebrew Mission; German Evangelical; Swedish Tabernacle, Swedish Mission, and Norwegian Bethania; Christ Chapel, Marie, Erie, and Railroad Chapels, and N. W. University Chapel, Evanston; also churches at Austin, Ravenswood, and other towns.

In addition to these and other meeting-places there were five large canvas tabernacles in constant use, which were moved from place to place, and which proved to be among the most effective arrangements to reach the masses of city residents and visitors. Another effective device was a gospel wagon, by means of which it was found possible to hold a number of open-air meetings in various parts of the city every day, with the happiest results.

By thus massing names of persons and places together on the printed page, the reader may get a more impressive idea of the extent and scope of the work that was carried forward, day after day, through the six months of the World's Fair. But the view is by no means complete or adequate. The management of the enterprise was a gigantic piece of work, and the machinery of organization was a gigantic system of adjusted workers. Never has Mr. Moody been so severely tested as to his organizing capacity, and skill and power of leadership, and probably never has he more fully measured up to the demands of any occasion or crisis of his evangelistic career. His experience was a new confirmation of the precious divine assurance he has learned so well: "My grace is sufficient for thee."

The amount of work and calculation involved in ar-

ranging for and carrying on the meetings, day by day, is
incalculable.   Success came not as a matter of course, or
by chance, but by downright hard, persistent work.   The
people were sought and brought to the meetings by keeping the one subject before them.   The newspapers, street-
cars, bill-boards, ticket-distributers, and personal solici-
tation were all brought into requisition to advertise the
meetings.   Nearly one and a half million tickets were
printed at one place alone, and the circulars and posters
who could count?   It was a grand, impressive object-
lesson on how to reach the people.   The inner history of
struggle and victory in providing for the financial part
of the colossal and costly enterprise will never be fully
known save to those in the inner circle of prevailing
prayer who bore the burden.

CHAPTER IX.

It was Mr. Moody's habit to meet his tired co-workers every night, in his room at the Bible Institute, to partake of refreshments, report the work of the day, and discuss the important interests of the meetings. As one by one the workers came in from their different preaching-places, churches, theaters, halls, tents, some near the midnight hour, the commander-in-chief had a word for each one, and nothing so cheered his heart and brightened his countenance as reports of souls saved and victories gained for the dear Lord Jesus Christ. Those nightly seasons of fellowship will be gratefully remembered by many as they live over again the trials and triumphs of that wonderful time. On Sunday nights, after the exhausting labors of the crowded days, the assembled workers always bowed with Mr. Moody in praise and thanksgiving to God before they retired to their places of rest.

Regular meetings were also held in the Bible Institute, when reports of work from the various preachers were called for. A glimpse of one such meeting, with Mr. Moody on the platform, catechising the workers, is given by a participant, as follows:

"Mr. Schiverea, what progress have you had the last week?"

"We have held a meeting every night, and children's meetings four afternoons in the week, with an average

43

of about 1000 at the night services and 300 during the day. God has inclined the hearts of the people to come, and not a few have decided for the Lord Jesus Christ. I have been in the city for four summers, and don't know of any season where God has opened the work with such grand prospects. The people are hungering for the simple gospel, and proving it by crowding the tent night after night. We have had some conversions of people who never go inside of church doors."

" What nationality are the people mostly ? "

"About nineteen nationalities are now represented in our meetings."

" Mr. Smith, what is the report from your tent ? "

" Last night we had one of the best meetings we have had yet. There has been sustained interest, and we have had large children's services Sunday afternoons. They have not been so large on the week-days. It is a hard neighborhood, three fourths of the people being Roman Catholics, but there has been quite an accession of Protestants during the last few years. Seventy percent. of our conversions in the past two weeks have been among Hollanders."

" Do you have many working-men ? "

" Yes, the back of the tent is filled with working-men night after night. Two men came every night for two weeks and studied the question very earnestly. I missed one of the men and went to the other and inquired for him. I found he had left his companion playing cards and come to the meeting. He decided for Christ. I sent him out for his companion and he brought him, but he did not decide for Christ at that time. However, he brought in another who did. It is an unchurched neighborhood, and it has been our work to bring out those who had no church connection."

"Are such churches as are there working in sympathy with you?"

"All the ministers of the Protestant churches, with one exception, have been on the platform nearly every night. I have received assistance from all the churches in the neighborhood. Our workers from here have been faithful, although it has been a long way to go."

"How does the work compare with previous summers?"

"I never saw better work."

"Do you have many World's Fair people?"

"Yes, ministers and others often come and introduce themselves."

"Mr. Schiverea, I forgot to ask you if you have the coöperation of the ministers?"

"Yes, somewhat. The church people come in."

"Mr. Atkinson, what about your tent?"

"We have a great deal to praise God for. I took the work in fear and trembling, never having been in charge of a tent before. Mrs. Capron gave me my old State Street workers, and the success is due to them through the blessing of God and prayer. The congregations have grown night after night. We have a children's meeting with an average attendance of 200, and an open-air meeting, conducted by Mr. Cantwell, where 500 people often hear the gospel. Two young ladies professed conversion, members of a Sunday-school class. They brought in another and she was converted, and the next night I saw them pleading and weeping with a fourth, and beseeching her to come to Christ. It is a respectable neighborhood. The churches have been stimulated by the meetings. An elder from a Presbyterian church stated that the previous Wednesday they had had the largest prayer-meeting they ever had had."

"What have you been doing, Mr. Dalgetty?"

"I have only been down in that tent a week. There was much disturbance among the boys. We made it a matter of serious prayer, and there has been an answer. Last night was the largest meeting we have had down there. There was a boy sitting near the front. I shook hands with him and asked him if he had trusted the Lord Jesus Christ. He answered, 'Yes.' 'How long?' 'One minute.' 'Are your sins pardoned?' 'Yes.' 'How do you know?' 'God says so.' 'Who spoke with you?' 'God.' He had decided during the preaching."

"Mr. Smith, will you report from the temperance meeting at Empire Theater?"

"There is good news from the temperance meeting. Last Saturday night close upon 200 signed the pledge. I don't know when it was ever so easy to get in spiritual work, as well as to have the pledge signed."

"What have you been doing at Institute Hall, Mr. Stephens?"

"We have been having three meetings every evening. We have an outdoor meeting, and a late meeting is held from ten till twelve every night, to catch the late passers-by."

"What proportion of the audience at the Empire Theater are men?"

"About two thirds. Most of them are from the crowd which hang about Canal Street—men out of work and drinking men."

"Are any of the drinking men being reached?"

"Yes, and we have had a song service in several saloons and have been well received."

"Mr. Pierson, we will hear what you have to tell us."

"The meetings at the Sunday-school Building have been going on for several weeks. An intelligent audience—among them are chair-rollers and Columbian guards out of employment and discouraged, so that their hearts are tender."

"Miss McClure, we would like to hear about the women's meeting at Empire Theater."

"We gathered together for prayer. There were several hundred there, and it was an easy meeting to lead, for it went of itself when it was once started. People were there from all over the country. One good woman who had come to Chicago to see the Fair had a son here who was not a Christian, and made up her mind to stay until he was. It seems to me it must have been easy for the evangelists to preach that night, for they were so upheld by prayer in the afternoon."

"What about the police work?"

"I don't know just how much is done in the city, but the ladies from our department have charge of five stations. They gather for a half-hour meeting before roll-call in the evening. Sometimes it is discouraging. The rooms are close, and the men would rather stay outside, but there are usually from ten to thirty men inside."

"Have you anything to add, Mrs. Capron?"

"I should like to have Miss Peters report the open-air meetings."

"These are the results of the cottage meetings of the winter. When the winter was over the people did not seem to want to have the meetings closed, so we planned an open-air meeting instead, and went out one afternoon with invitations. We began singing, and many whom I had not seen before began to gather around, and seemed greatly interested. We rejoiced because the meeting was so quiet, as a mission in that place had had to close because of disturbance by the boys. I spoke to the boy who was the leader, and the next time he came, and afterward said, 'Wasn't I quiet to-night?'"

"Is Mr. McNeill here?"

Mr. McNeill responded: "We have had very good meetings at Englewood Church, an audience of from 1500 to 2000."

The reports, the comments, the questions asked and answered, the suggestions concerning work and workers, the spirit of faith, zeal, and enthusiasm, made these meetings exceedingly interesting and profitable.

There is one other item with respect to Mr. Moody's management of the meetings which must not be overlooked. He believes that it is a religious duty and privilege, and a necessary condition of health and effectiveness, to rest one day in seven. The writer has repeatedly heard him ascribe his own freshness and vigor and sustained working capacity to his observance of a seventh-day rest. Accordingly, his plan of evangelistic campaign must provide for a seventh-day rest for himself and for all his workers, while the Sabbath is the busiest and most exhausting day of the seven. Monday was the day set apart for this purpose for the majority of the workers, and those who were obliged to work on that day were released from labor on Saturday, or some other day.

CHAPTER X.

AMONG the most notable of the large meetings held during the early part of the campaign were those in the Mammoth Forepaugh's Circus tent and in Tattersall's huge barracks-like hall, on the south side. In the former place two meetings were held, on two successive Sundays in June. The circus tent covered an immense area, with 10,000 seats and an arena capable of accommodating 10,000 more. In the center of the arena a rude platform was erected for the speakers and a few of the singers, while the rest of the song corps were massed around them. An observer describes the scene in few words as follows: "The surroundings were the usual circus furniture—ropes, trapezes, gaudy decorations, etc., while in an adjoining canvas building was a large menagerie, including eleven elephants. Clowns, grooms, circus riders, men, women, and children, drinking and betting men, pickpockets, all gathered, we were informed, into this unique assembly. What a crowd it was! Men, women, and children, 18,000 of them, and on a Sunday morning, too! Whether the gospel was ever before preached under such circumstances I know not, but it was wonderful, to ear and eye alike. The sight of the vast sea of faces was at once glad and solemn. By half-past nine the choir took their places in front of an audience already vast in extent, although tickets were available for half an hour, yet be-

49

fore that entrance was free to all comers. Be it understood, however, that tickets were not in use to keep people out, but to get them in. In other words, they had been placed in the hands of all who would accept them in train or street-car, road or sidewalk, store or hotel, wheresoever the feet of willing workers had been able to gain admittance for the purpose.

"After nearly an hour of singing, individual and congregational, which swept like the voice of the ocean across the field of heads, Mr. Moody rose before probably the largest audience he had ever been called upon to face, and delivered one of those addresses, burning with earnestness, pathos, and love, which, owned by the Spirit of God, have drawn so many not only under the sound of the gospel, but also under its power. His text was, 'The Son of Man is come to seek and to save that which was lost,' and his address was a pathetic appeal to sinners to turn to God, delivered with unction and tenderness. Profoundly moved by the vast throng before him, he spoke as though realizing that many of his auditors might never again hear the gospel call. The silence became intense. Closer and closer pressed the people. Broken by the power of the Holy Spirit, the tears rolled unheeded and unwiped from faces to which tears were doubtless strangers. Numbers of young men gave way to their feelings, heedless of who might be looking on. Toward the close of his address there was a slight disturbance, and Mr. Moody found that the cause of it was a 'lost child.' He quickly had the little girl brought to the platform, and by holding her up to the audience made an effort to discover her parents. In this he was successful. While the father was making his way to the platform Mr. Moody went on with his address, and when the anxious man reached the preacher's side Mr. Moody placed the child in her father's

arms, and said, 'This is what Jesus Christ came to do.
He came to seek and save sinners, and restore them to
their Heavenly Father's embrace.' This unusual kind of
illustration came home to many with much power.

"After Mr. Moody's address, Rev. John McNeill had a
turn. He spoke in his own happy, simple style, his fine
voice sweeping away back to the farthest corner of the
amphitheater, and he, too, in his own characteristic way,
presented the truth of Christ from another standpoint,
but directed to the same goal. And thus, in the mouths
of two witnesses, and by the fervent prayers of hundreds
of hearts, was that truth established before a throng
which, for diversity of appearance, incongruity of the surroundings, but at the same time closeness of attention,
stood, perhaps, unique in the annals of gospel work. A
similar service, held the following Sabbath, was addressed
by Messrs. Moody, McNeill, Schiverea, and Torrey. This
occasion, having only been advertised for two days, was
not so largely attended, but that 9000 persons should have
heard the powerful presentation of the love of God which
his servants gave was much to be thankful for."

When Mr. Moody was arranging for this circus-tent
meeting, one of the circus men, with an air of incredulity
and contempt, asked if he thought he could get 3000
hearers there. The man learned at least one lesson before the day was over. So also did the manager of the
circus, who granted Mr. Moody the use of the tent for
Sunday morning, but reserved it for the afternoon and
evening, expecting to draw immense crowds to his performances. It was a revelation to him when he saw in
the morning from 15,000 to 18,000 persons listening to
songs and sermons, and so few coming to see his performances in afternoon and evening that he had to give up
Sunday exhibitions altogether. The manager, moreover,

frankly stated that Sunday performances were an experiment with him, and that he would not try it again. He then asked Mr. Moody for an evangelist to travel with him, offering the use of his tent on Sundays for gospel meetings, and promising to pay all expenses of the arrangement.

When Mr. Moody announced the meeting to be held in Tattersall's Hall, with its capacity of from 10,000 to 15,000 people, he said: "We've got something better than Buffalo Bill, and we must get a bigger audience than he does." Concerning this meeting, Mr. Morgan writes: "Considerable effort was obviously necessary to secure a full audience in view of the multitudinous worldly attractions rife in the city on Sunday and week-day alike. Accordingly twenty men visited the back parts of the city for several hours on the Saturday night and Sunday morning, distributing tickets of admission from house to house, in drinking and gambling saloons, brothels, and in the streets. On the whole, and especially considering the low type of places visited, a very favorable reception was accorded, and it was especially gratifying to find the unqualified respect in which the evangelist is held even by those whose business suffers at his hands. The individual testimonies to this were quite as forcible as the splendid muster of men of every class who throng every building in which he is announced to preach.

"An amusing incident occurred during this district visitation. A saloon-keeper, becoming enraged at the invasion of his premises for such a purpose, tore up all the tickets he could grab from the hands of his customers, and summoned a policeman to eject the perpetrator of the outrage. A burly form in blue promptly seized the offender, who, however, by dint of some facetious remark, raised a laugh at the officer's expense. This dispelled the

solemnity of the occasion, and he followed up his advantage by asking the saloon-keeper whether, as he objected
to his customers going to the meeting, he would not represent them by going himself. 'Ah,' he said, 'you wouldn't
welcome me if I did!' 'Indeed we would,' was the reply;
'see, here's a special ticket' (writing a pass to a reserved
seat on a visiting-card). 'Then I'll go,' he responded;
'that's a bet!' And he kept his word. Needless to add,
the visitor was allowed to repeat his distribution among
the customers, and the policeman, somewhat disappointed,
resumed his beat alone. In another saloon the keeper
besought the visitor not to make a fool of himself, which
gave rise to a discussion between himself and his wife
(who, standing behind the bar, had already accepted a
ticket), during which the distribution was continued without further interruption.

"As to the meeting itself, there was a splendid con-
course of 8000 people, who listened with closest attention
to an address longer in point of time than is Mr. Moody's
wont; and although the hall did not afford facilities for
an after-meeting, about 500 young men responded to an
invitation to remain awhile at the close. Many of these
proved to be strangers in the city, whom Mr. Moody invited to coöperate in or to attend the various services to
be held during the summer for their own blessing and
that of others. Such an audience as had assembled was
the more remarkable, seeing that the evangelist had already addressed 4000 persons in a large theater during
the forenoon, and that, to say nothing of other attractions,
the Fair was open all day."

CHAPTER XI.

WE will help the reader to see the bare skeleton of a single day's work of the evangelistic forces by setting before him, first, a bird's-eye view of the labors of one Sunday in the middle of the campaign, and, second, a specimen program of another Sunday in the last month, and the week following it, which will show one style of advertising, and also mark the extension and enlargement of the work, as compared with the former.

Sunday, in the evangelistic work, like every other day at the Bible Institute, began with seasons of devotion in both departments, where the workers refreshed themselves with fellowship in song and prayer and the Word of God, girding themselves for their coming labors. Mr. Moody was announced to preach in the Haymarket Theater in the morning. The announcement was the signal for a great rush, and an hour before the time a crowd was at the door. Some 3000 people were packed into the spacious building, while thousands failed to get in. The outside crowd were invited to enter the Standard Theater, three blocks away, and soon 2500 souls filled that building, and still other hundreds failed to get in. Mr. Moody preached with telling effect to the great multitude in the Haymarket. An observer estimates that about 7000 people surged into and about the two theaters at the morning service.

At 4 P.M. Mr. Moody and Major Whittle addressed 2500

people in the crowded Standard Theater, many of whom had waited there since the morning service to get the opportunity to see and hear the evangelist and his associate. The Word was with power and manifest effect. In the evening Mr. Moody had another service, preaching to an audience of 2200 in the First Congregational Church.

Rev. John McNeill spoke twice in churches too small to contain the crowds that flocked to hear him. In the morning he addressed a congregation in the First Presbyterian Church, when the doors had to be locked against the outside pressure after the service had begun. In the evening, in the large Immanuel Baptist Church, some 2200 people listened to his sermon, while hundreds were turned away.

Dr. A. B. Simpson, of New York, preached with power, morning and evening, to congregations of 1800 in Chicago Avenue Church.

Dr. C. I. Scofield, of Dallas, Tex., conducted three services; in the morning he addressed a crowd that packed the Standard Theater from the overflow of the Haymarket; in the afternoon he spoke to an audience of 2000 at another place; and in the evening in the Forty-first Street Presbyterian Church.

Dr. J. Munro Gibson, of London, spoke in the morning in the Forty-first Street Presbyterian Church to 1200 people, and in the evening in the Second Presbyterian Church to about the same number.

Rev. R. A. Torrey addressed an audience of all kinds in the Standard Theater in the evening, and many a hard heart was pierced by the truth.

Major D. W. Whittle spoke in the afternoon, after Mr. Moody, in the Standard Theater meeting, and in the evening at his tent at North Clark and Roscoe Streets, when salvation came to many.

Mr. Ferd. Schiverea had a full day in his wonderful tent-work at North and Washtenaw Avenues. In the morning he spoke to a crowd of 500; in the afternoon he had 1000 hearers, and in the evening 2000, a great wave of human beings that poured in and over and all around his tent.

Mr. Merton Smith had an audience of 1000 in and around his tent at West Fourteenth and Paulina Streets.

Mr. J. M. Scroggie, a Scottish evangelist, addressed an audience of 700 in Immanuel Presbyterian Church.

Mr. F. T. Pierson, aided effectively by his wife, who sings the gospel, conducted three services—two in the Columbian Sunday-school Building, with audiences of 700 and 800, and another in Englewood Y. M. C. A. Building, with 500 hearers.

Messrs. W. Dalgetty and Ralph Atkinson had their usual evening tent services, one at Twenty-sixth Street and Wentworth Avenue, and the other at West Chicago Avenue and Lincoln Street, both tents filled to overflowing with congregations of 400 and 900.

Mr. Richard Hill, another Scotch evangelist, spoke with power to a large audience in the Campbell Park Presbyterian Church, and not without effect.

Rev. Niclaus Boldt, a young German preacher from St. Paul, held the closing one of a week's services, in the German language, in Christ Chapel, with a congregation of about 500 deeply impressed hearers.

Rev. A. Skoogsbergh, a Swedish evangelist, preached in his own language, morning and evening, to congregations of 800, in the Bethania Norwegian Church.

An afternoon service in the Bohemian language was conducted, when about 500 Bohemians heard the gospel in their own language.

In Major Whittle's tent a remarkable meeting for children was conducted by Miss Bessie Tyson. About 600 people were present to share in the blessings of the hour.

At Institute Hall, in the heart of Chicago's dark places, three services were held in afternoon and evening, continuing till nearly midnight. An aggregate of between 700 and 800 people were there brought under the influence of the gospel.

At Bethesda Congregational Church, one of the Institute workers conducted a meeting. Mrs. E. M. Whittemore, of New York, had a memorable service among the 400 prisoners in the jail. In the afternoon she also conducted an impressive consecration meeting in the Moody Church, attended by about 300 persons.

Some of the Institute workers conducted a meeting of about 600 people at Colonel Clarke's well-known mission.

Throughout the day over twenty mission services were held by other Institute workers, by which nearly 2000 persons were reached with gospel influences.

The gospel wagon, manned by evangelists Davis and Higgins, and part of the time also by Mr. Wm. Robertson, of Edinburgh, with a force of trained Institute workers, was employed morning, afternoon, and evening, reaching an aggregate of 1200 people with the gospel in song, sermon, and testimony.

About 300 people were addressed in an open-air service held in the evening.

In all these meetings the gospel singers took a prominent and very important part, especially in the great theater gatherings. There the strongest forces of singers were massed. Messrs. Towner, Stebbins, Jacobs, Burke, Atkinson, Mrs. Pierson, strong male choirs, four male quartets, and scores of other singers proclaimed the glad tidings in thrilling song. Trained Christian workers, male and female, from the Bible Institute, assisted in every service.

It is impossible to tabulate the results of one Sunday's work for souls. Hundreds professed faith in Christ. Many will carry their new life and testimony far and wide into the various places of their abode, and much fruit shall be found after many days.

ONE SPECIMEN PROGRAM.

BIBLE INSTITUTE.

(80 Institute Place, near La Salle and Chicago Avenues.)

Sabbath Program, October 8th.

Mr. Moody preaches in the Haymarket Theater, 169 West Madison Street, at 10.30, and in Immanuel Baptist Church, Michigan Avenue, near Twenty-third Street, at 3 and 7. Plymouth Congregational Church, Michigan Avenue, near Twenty-sixth Street, at 8.

Rev. John McNeill, in the Columbia Theater, Monroe Street, near Dearborn, at 11, and in Central Music Hall at 3 and 8. Mr. Burke sings.

Mr. Henry Varley, of London, in Hooley's Theater, Randolph Street, near La Salle, at 10.30. Mr. Stebbins sings. In Standard Theater, Jackson and Halsted Streets, at 3, and in Second Baptist Church, Morgan and Monroe Streets, at 7.30.

Rev. A. T. Pierson, D.D., in Second Presbyterian Church, Michigan Avenue and Twentieth Street, at 10.45 and 7.45, and in Plymouth Congregational Church, Michigan Avenue, near Twenty-sixth Street, at 3.30.

L. W. Munhall, in Oakwood M. E. Church, Oakwood Boulevard and Langley Avenue, at 10.45 and 7.45.

Mr. Chas. Inglis, of London, in Chicago Avenue Church, corner La Salle and Chicago Avenues, at 10.30, and in the People's Institute, Van Buren and Oakley Streets, at 3.30 and 7.30. Mr. Towner sings.

Rev. Jas. H. Brookes, D.D., of St. Louis, in the Second Baptist Church, Morgan and West Monroe Streets, at 10.45; in First Congregational Church, Ann Street and Washington Boulevard, at 3.30; and in Chicago Avenue Church at 7.30.

Rev. George C. Needham, in Langley Avenue Baptist Church, Langley Avenue, near Seventy-first Street, at 10.45 and 7.45. Union service in the afternoon at 3; every week-night at 8.

R. A. Torrey (superintendent of the Bible Institute), Bible-class in Chicago Avenue Church at 3 P.M.

Rev. T. B. Hyde, in Model Sunday-school Building, Fifty-seventh Street and Stony Island Avenue, at 10.30 and 7.30. Mr. H. W. Stough sings.

Mr. John H. Elliott, in Belden Avenue Baptist Church, Belden Avenue and Halsted Street, at 10.45 and 7.45.

Major-General O. O. Howard and Major Whittle, Fourth Baptist Church, Ashland and Monroe Streets, at 10.45; Standard Theater at 8.

Rev. C. O. Jones, of Tennessee, in Auburn Park M. E. Church, 622 Sixty-ninth Street, at 10.45 and 7.45.

Mr. D. W. Potter preaches in Epworth Hotel Tabernacle, Fifty-ninth Street and Monroe Avenue, at 10.45 and 7.45.

Mr. Robert Speer, in Hotel Endeavor Tabernacle, Seventy-fifth Street and Bond Avenue, at 10.45 and 7.45.

Rev. H. C. Trumbull, in First Congregational Church at 7.45.

Mr. Ralph Atkinson, at Blue Island, Ill., in M. E. Church at 10.45; Y. M. C. A. at 4; and in the Congregational Church at 7.45.

Miss B. B. Tyson, of Washington, D. C., holds a Children's Service in the People's Institute at 10.30.

R. A. Hadden, of St. Paul, Minn., in Y. M. C. A., 148 East Madison Street, in the evening.

Mr. L. P. Rowland, at Wheaton, Ill., M. E. Church.

Week-Day Announcements, October 9–14.

Mr. Moody, at 8 P.M. Monday, in the Railroad Chapel, Thirty-ninth and Dearborn Streets. Tuesday, Epworth Hotel Tabernacle.

Major Whittle, Tuesday and Wednesday in the Railroad Chapel at 8 P.M.

Rev. John McNeill and Mr. Burke at 8 P.M. Monday, in the Model Sunday-school Building. Tuesday, in the Standard Theater. Wednesday, at Lake Forest, Ill. Thursday, in Railroad Chapel.

L. W. Munhall, in Englewood, First Presbyterian Church, Sixty-fourth Street and Yale Avenue, at 8 P.M.

Rev. Geo. C. Needham, D.D., in Langley Avenue Baptist Church, Langley Avenue, near Seventy-first Street, at 8 P.M.

Mr. Henry Varley, of London, in Willard Hall, The Woman's Temple, Monroe and La Salle Streets, 12 to 1 o'clock daily. Saturday, at 8 P.M., in the Standard Theater. Monday, Epworth Hotel Tabernacle, 8 P.M.

Miss B. B. Tyson, of Washington, D. C., holds children's meetings in the tents during the afternoons.

Central Music Hall, State and Randolph Streets. Monday: special meeting, 10 to 2 o'clock. All the preachers will be present. Mr. Moody will preach the sermon he preached the night of the Chicago fire, October 8, 1871. Tuesday to Saturday, Mr. Moody and Rev. John McNeill speak daily from 11 to 1 o'clock.

Mr. Chas. Inglis and Mr. Towner, People's Institute, every night at 8 o'clock.

Dr. A. T. Pierson, in the Fourth Baptist Church, Ashland and Monroe Streets, Tuesday to Friday, at 8 P.M.

Model Sunday-school Building, Fifty-seventh Street and Stony Island Avenue. Meetings every night at 7.30. Rev. T. B. Hyde in charge. Mr. R. C. Marquis leads the singing.

President C. A. Blanchard, of Wheaton College, in the Model Sunday-school Building, on Thursday, at 7.30 P.M.

Institute Hall, 191 West Madison Street. Gospel meetings every night at 7.30 and 10 o'clock. Mr. C. H. Stevens in charge.

The Bible Institute, 80 Institute Place, near La Salle and Chicago Avenues. *Lectures every morning (except Monday)*: 9 o'clock, Tuesday to Friday, Mr. Henry Varley; 11 o'clock, Tuesday to Friday, Dr. J. H. Brookes, of St. Louis; 11 o'clock, Saturday, R. A. Torrey.

Standard Theater, Jackson and Halsted Streets. R. A. Torrey speaks every night at 8. Mr. Atkinson sings.

Five Tents, meetings at 8 P.M.:

No. 1. Center Avenue and Orchard Street. Rev. C. O. Jones, of Tennessee, in charge. Mr. F. H. Jacobs sings.

No. 2. Corner Milwaukee and Powell Avenues. Ferd. Schiverea preaches. Mr. Wellicome leads the singing.

No. 3. Paulina and Walnut Streets. Merton Smith preaches. Children's meetings daily at 4 P.M.

No. 4. Archer Avenue and Twenty-third Place. W. Dalgetty preaches. Institute Quartet sing.

No. 5. West Chicago Avenue and Lincoln Street. Major Cole preaches. Mr. Wolf leads the singing.

CHAPTER XII.

At the risk of some repetition, but with the assurance of gaining a fuller, clearer view, we transfer to these pages two brief summary statements from competent observers and participants—bird's-eye glimpses of the work during one of the earlier months of the campaign. The first is from Rev. A. J. Gordon, D.D., pastor of the Clarendon Street Baptist Church, Boston, who was associated with Mr. Moody in the work during the month of July. Writing for his own paper, the *Watchword*, Dr. Gordon says, with special reference to the July work:

"A man's work often furnishes the best character-sketch of himself which can possibly be drawn. We therefore give an outline of Mr. Moody's summer campaign in Chicago as a kind of full-length portrait of the evangelist himself. Let the reader be reminded that it is in the months of July and August, when many city pastors are summering, that this recreation scheme of Mr. Moody's is carried on after his hard year's campaign in England and America.

"Four of the largest churches in different parts of the city are held for Sunday evenings and various week-evening services. Two theaters, the Empire and the Haymarket, located in crowded centers, are open on Sundays, and the former on every week-night, and they are not infrequently filled to their utmost capacity while the gospel is preached and sung. Five tents are pitched in localities where the unprivileged and non-church-going multitudes live. In these services are held nightly, and as we have visited them we have found them always filled with such, for the most part, as do not attend any place of Protestant worship. A hall in the heart of the city is kept open night after night, the services continuing far on to the morning hours, while earnest workers are busily fishing within and without for drunkards and harlots. Two gospel wagons are moving about dispensing the Word of Life to such as may be induced to stop and listen, and the workers estimate that 1000 or more are thus reached daily of those who would not enter a church or mission hall.

"Daily lectures are given at the Institute for the instruction in the Bible of the students, Christian workers, ministers, missionaries, and others who wish to attend. The large hall in which these lectures are given, seating comfortably 350, is always filled. During July there were thirty-eight preachers, evangelists, and singers, and other agents coöperating in the work, and their labors are supplemented by an endless variety of house-to-house and highway-and-hedge effort by the 250 students in residence in the Institute.

"'We shall beat the World's Fair,' said Mr. Moody good-naturedly, as we arrived on the ground. With malice toward none and charity toward all, this is what he set out to do, viz., to furnish such gospel attractions, by supplementing the churches and coöperating with them, that the multitudes visiting the city might be kept in attendance on religious services on Sunday instead of attending the Fair. So it has been. Mr. Moody estimates that from 30,000 to 40,000 people have been reached by his special Sunday evangelistic services. This multiplied by seven days easily foots up about 100,000 brought weekly within reach of the gospel. The World's Fair has been closed on Sunday for want of attendance, but the religious services are daily growing. Every good opening for the gospel is readily seized. When Forepaugh's great circus tent had been set up in the city Mr. Moody tried to secure it for Sunday. He was granted the use of it for a Sabbath morning service, but as the manager expected Sunday in Chicago to be a great harvest day, he reserved the tent on the afternoon and evening for his own performances. Fifteen thousand people came to hear the simple gospel preached and sung at the morning service. The circus, however, was so poorly attended in the afternoon and evening that Sunday exhibitions were soon abandoned. More than that, the manager said he had never been in the habit of giving performances on Sunday and should not attempt it again, and he offered, if Mr. Moody would appoint an evangelist to travel with him, to open his tent thereafter on Sundays for gospel meetings, and be responsible for all expenses.

"It was the same with the theaters. At first they declined to allow religious services on Sunday. Their performances on that day not having proved as successful as they anticipated, now Mr. Moody can hire almost any one which he wishes to secure.

"Eulogy and biographical encomiums upon living men are undesirable, and the writer has risked the displeasure of his friend in putting so much into print concerning him. But we may hope that what we have written will awaken serious reflections in the minds of ministers and laymen alike concerning the problem of summer work and summer success for the gospel in our great cities.

"We may also hope that a stronger faith in the divine administration and mighty efficiency of the Holy Ghost may be hereby inspired. We have no idea that the large and extensive religious enterprises which we have been describing are due alone to the superior natural endowments of the evangelist. For years in his meetings and conferences we have heard him emphasize the presence and power of the Holy Ghost in the worker as the one and indispensable condition of success. It must be that where the Spirit has been so constantly recognized and honored he has been doing invisibly and irresistibly much of the great work which human judgment attributes to the man who is the chosen agent."

The second statement we quote is from Rev. J. Munro Gibson, D.D., formerly of Chicago, now of London, who spent about a month in Chicago, preaching and lecturing in connection with Mr. Moody's campaign. On his return to his London congregation he gave them a bird's-eye view of what he had seen of the Chicago work, speaking somewhat as follows :

"While the Fair was deserted on Sundays, the churches were crowded. Of course, wherever Mr. Moody or Mr. McNeill preached there was no getting in, unless you went an hour or more before the time. But even with only an ordinary preacher there would be a full church, and that not in the morning only, but also at the evening service, which it is specially difficult to keep up in Chicago, as I remember by experience. On week-nights, too, the people would come in numbers. Be it remembered that there was not only the Fair, with its marvelous illuminations, to contend with, but there were likewise the attractions in the city suited to all tastes—from the great congresses on the questions of the day to the lowest variety show. One would think that in these circumstances it would be almost impossible to keep up the attendance on a week-night at a religious service. Quite the contrary. The

churches had their prayer-meetings all through the dog-
days, and sometimes when it was least expected there
would be a crowd. One Wednesday evening I was asked
to take a service at a new town on the other side of the
Fair grounds. When I got there I was surprised to find
that instead of calling the meeting in some small lecture-
hall, as I had expected, they had opened the largest church
in the place. But the event justified what had appeared
to me their unreasonable expectation, for not only was
the building crowded to suffocation, but very many had
to go away. And lest you may suppose that I had anything to do with this, I may say that on comparing notes
afterward with one who had been doing the same thing
in another suburb, I found that he had had precisely the
same experience.

"But the regular services were not all. Mr. Moody
had not only done what he could to stir up the churches
to special activity during the great opportunity of the
Fair, but had made special arrangements for extraordinary services. He got possession of some of the theaters
in central positions for evangelistic services. Sometimes
he himself preached in them, but the success did not de-
pend on his presence, for when he was away at Northfield
you would find some able lieutenant like Professor Torrey
of the Bible Institute, Mr. Scroggie of Glasgow, or Mr.
Varley of London, at the Haymarket, or the Empire, or
the Standard Theater, preaching the gospel to a full house,
and drawing the gospel net at the close.

"These theater services were, as I have said, in central
places; but farther out, though still in the crowded parts,
there were tents, as many as five, where the gospel was
preached night after night. I was only able to attend
one of these services; it was in a large tent, holding, I
should think, about a thousand people, and so brilliantly

lighted that the street, with its arc lights, seemed dark in
comparison. There Mr. Schiverea, a man who years ago
was rescued from evil ways by Mr. Moody, and who is
now a preacher of great power with singular adaptation
for reaching the common people, was holding forth to a
thoroughly interested audience, which almost filled the tent
in every part. It was a Saturday night, and the animated
appearance of the throng in the tent presented a singular
and most encouraging contrast to the deserted look of the
saloons and places of entertainment in the street close by.
It was the liveliest place I saw that night, and I traveled
a good distance along the streets.

"The tent-meetings are held in the evening hours, but
when they are closed the work of the day is not yet done,
for if you go to Institute Hall on the west side you may
be in time for the ten-o'clock meeting there—not a large
and crowded meeting like the others, but specially interesting in its way; for to this place the students of the
Bible Institute, and others working with them in the
streets and lanes, will bring, by ones or twos, some of the
very lowest of the people. There is a prayer-meeting
earlier in the evening, and now from ten o'clock till midnight this hard and discouraging but Christ-like work will
be going on.

"But, now, is not that enough? Surely it ought to be;
surely there will be no attempt at morning work in so
busy a time. Yes; there is more than an attempt, for it
is quite a success. All through the season there have been
held two morning meetings at the main Institute buildings
on the North side, one at nine and the other at eleven;
and now, in the month of August, are they closed for the
heat? No; they are crowded out of the lecture-room, to
take refuge in Mr. Moody's large church. They do not
fill it, of course, but even the nine-o'clock meeting looks

respectable in it, and the eleven-o'clock meeting, which is taken by Mr. Moody himself after his return from North-field, nearly fills it, with the exception of the galleries, which are not open. These morning meetings are for the special benefit, first of students at the Bible Institute, and next of the Christian people who wish to have their enthusiasm kindled to take part in the aggressive work, which goes on, as we have seen, in the evening and into the night."

CHAPTER XIII.

PROBABLY nowhere was there deeper interest felt in the Chicago evangelistic movement than in Mr. Moody's home town of Northfield, and by the Christian people gathered there during the summer season. When Dr. Gordon arrived there on the 1st of August, fresh from the Chicago work, there was an eager desire to learn all about it, to which he made response by giving a morning address to the Christian Conference, then in session, on "Mr. Moody's Work in Chicago." Some extracts from this address will afford further glimpses of some aspects of the work, and form the fitting prelude of what followed its presentation.

"You will remember," said Dr. Gordon, "that I came to this conference directly from Chicago, where I have been during the month of July assisting Mr. Moody as best I could in the great work he has undertaken for that city in this centennial year. I have no doubt that universal joy has been experienced among Christians throughout this country at the tidings that came two Sundays ago that the Fair was closed. It is closed practically and theoretically, though it was opened last Sunday in a very limited way. Now I do not hesitate to say, having been there a whole month and having observed the work very carefully, that the closing of the Fair is very much related to the church and evangelistic work which has been going on in that city during the past two months. A single

statement may make this much of this assertion obvious:
The last Sunday I was there the *Inter-Ocean* gave the
largest attendance that could be counted on the Fair
grounds as less than 30,000. Mr. Moody estimated that
on a recent Sunday there were gathered in connection with
his evangelistic services 40,000 people, while the regular
church services were also remarkably well attended.

"Now I like the spirit in which our beloved friend and
leader undertook this work. Some said, 'Let us boycott
the Fair;' others said, 'Let us appeal to the law and put
in money enough to prosecute its managers and compel
them to shut it up.' But our friend, Mr. Moody, said:
'Now let us open so many preaching-places and present
so many attractions that the people from all parts of the
world will come and hear the gospel,' and that is actually
what has happened.

"There are four churches that have opened to the dis-
posal of Mr. Moody, three of them among the largest in
the city, where meetings have been held Sunday evenings,
and they have always been filled. There are five tents
placed in the most strategic points for reaching the non-
church-going masses, and as I have visited them I have
found them always filled, and largely with those who are
not accustomed to be found in any Protestant places of
worship. Then two theaters, the Haymarket and the Empire, have been leased. I was present at the opening of
the Haymarket Theater, and the first Sunday the floor
was filled and the second gallery. Two Sundays after
the Empire Theater was filled and crowded in every part.
Last Sunday these theaters were so crowded that the people could not get in, and in the Empire Theater, at the
close of the services, after the gospel had been preached
an appeal was made for those who desired to seek the
Lord, and 500 people rose to their feet.

"Now this is what I often found to be true: that these congregations were made up of people from every part of the United States and Canada, and I may say from every part of the globe; everybody that has come up to the World's Fair is represented in these meetings—a great mass of people brought together from every nation and every race in the world, and preachers are brought together who can speak to them in their own tongue. So it is a remarkable movement. I remember that a friend suggested to Mr. Spurgeon that such a great preacher as he ought not to confine his ministry to London, but that he ought to make a tour around the world and preach to everybody; and Mr. Spurgeon replied, 'I can just stand in my place in London, and let the world come to me;' and so they did, as a matter of fact. And so this World's Fair is a great opportunity because all the world is present in Chicago, and being there, they come to hear the gospel. I consider it one of the most blessed triumphs of the grace of God that on these Sundays the people are attending church and listening to the Word of God instead of going for recreation. Now that is the right way to conquer: not by violence, not by law, not by threatening, but by a counter-attraction, by offering something better.

"I have made this statement in order that we may praise God that such advantage is being taken of this great occasion that will never come again. We shall never again see such an event. I need not say that the Fair is magnificent; it is a dazzling alabaster city set on the lake. People are there from every part of the earth; and next to that architectural wonder, and the marvelous display of art and science and beauty of every sort, I consider that the most striking thing in that city to-day is the evangelistic work that is going on."

Having presented the work of the evangelists in considerable detail to the deeply interested conference, and knowing its enormous expense and need of support, Dr. Gordon continued:

"I have been here to every conference, at least during some part of the session, since they began. I was here when that first building stood alone, and this field where we stand now was a rough and stony pasture. Now I remember that during these years Mr. Moody has appealed to the people for all sorts of good things, but always refused to have any aid for himself in his work; when it has been suggested he has declined. Now he is absent, and we can take advantage of his absence to-day. I know that this is a very heavy enterprise which he has undertaken, and we know very well that we have struck very hard times financially, when it is very difficult to get money. I am going to request now that you will make an offering for that work, because you know it is a centennial work that belongs to the whole world. We have an interest in the World's Fair; it is not a local, but a cosmopolitan, affair. I know that every person here, and some that are not here that will come, and some who were here and have gone, when they hear about it, will say: 'I should delight to make an offering as a testimony of my affectionate regard for our leader, who is necessarily absent on account of his work, to assist him in carrying on this magnificent World's Fair enterprise.' I am sure I shall be approved in taking the responsibility of making this appeal."

Mr. H. M. Moore, of Boston, followed Dr. Gordon with an appeal for such an offering as had been proposed. He said: "As I have come up to this convention, I have noticed a great many familiar faces here and there, persons whose names I could not always recall, but who I knew had received a blessing at Northfield. Now what do you come back here for year after year? I think you come, as I do, because you said in your very heart of hearts that Northfield meets a felt want in your soul. Like Dr. Gordon, I have had the privilege of being here at every convention from the time the tent was pitched out beyond East Hall and there was only the one building, and I come here because I feel the need as you do.

"Now during all these years, how our minds go back from time to time! We remember standing here on this platform when John G. Woolley gave that wonderful temperance address, and Mr. Moody said that a man who could talk like that ought to be sent out through all this country, and proposed that we raise money enough to send him out. Over $3000 was raised, and since that time God has taken care of him, and we all know what a great work he has done. We also remember how Mr. Shelton stood here, telling us of the needs of the Indians on the frontier, illustrating it with the affecting story of the Indian who came one hundred and fifty miles, asking if some one would not come to his tribe and his people and tell them of Jesus Christ, and how they could not find a man to go; and we remember how Mr. Moody raised nearly $3000 to plant a mission among the Indians. Then in two years Mr. Shelton came back and Mr. Moody said: 'It is a shame if we cannot take care of our own children,' and so he raised some more money for him. And when Bishop Thoburn was here Mr. Moody raised $3000 and planted missions in India, and the next year Bishop Thoburn came back and told of 20,000 souls converted that year through the money that had been given.

"Now, as Dr. Gordon has said, here is a mighty enterprise, which Mr. Moody has organized with his thirty-three to thirty-six helpers, besides the 220 students who are also helping in this mighty work. Men are being touched by the power of the Word through the Spirit of God, and are drawn there, and are brought to know and believe in Jesus Christ.

"The work is not for Chicago alone; it is a work for this round globe, for there are people from every country and nation and tribe. It seems to me, money given to that work is given direct for foreign missions, for I believe we will find that Mr. Moody never has engaged in as great a work (except the organizing of these schools here, which I believe to be the greatest work of his life) as he is doing there in Chicago, because those men, those foreigners that have come there and have been converted, are going back home to be missionaries of the cross; and I believe in that great day, by and by, when you and I are gathered with the redeemed, there will be many who will gather and sing the song of Him who has bought us with his own precious blood, who will say, 'It was at the World's Fair in '93 that I learned for the first time that Jesus Christ died to save men.'

"Now it does seem to me, when we think of what Mr. Moody has done for others, and never asked for one thing for his own work, that we ought to feel it a blessed privilege to help on this work."

It was not necessary to urge the people to contribute to the support of the work of which they had heard such good report. The cause made its own appeal, and the response was prompt, hearty, and generous. In sums varying from one to five hundred dollars the pledges came in from all parts of the hall, and in half an hour over $6000 was reported. A telegram announcing the good news was promptly sent to Mr. Moody at Chicago. When the telegram arrived it was a time of special need and perplexity. The finances were unusually low, and $4000 was needed to meet present obligations. Mr. Moody, in speaking of the experience, said: "I called a meeting of the leaders to consider what was to be done to meet our obligations. I did not like to speak to them of money matters, for they had so much else to attend to. While gathered together the telegram came from Northfield stating that $6000 had been raised to carry on the work, and I cannot tell you how welcome it was, or how grateful I am to those who gave it. I recognize it not as coming from them, but from the Lord."

Several days later the Northfield contribution was increased to $10,000, many of the former givers doubling their gifts, while many new-comers contributed gifts ranging from fifty cents to five hundred dollars. It was a timely act, for it strengthened the hands of the leaders in Chicago, and cheered them on in the great and difficult work they had undertaken.

CHAPTER XIV.

A HAYMARKET MEETING.

Repeated reference has been made to the theaters as centers of operation in spreading the gospel. It was well known that the attempt to gather congregations for religious services and for soul-saving in such buildings, in the midst of a very hell of saloons and vile resorts of all kinds, was by many regarded as a daring, if not foolhardy experiment. But God from the first set his seal of power upon the effort and honored the faith, love, and zeal of his servants. Thousands upon thousands of people, unused to song and prayer and gospel preaching, were in those places brought under the gracious influence of the Word and Spirit of God, and many found there the way of a new life in Jesus Christ. There, too, many were reached and reclaimed who had wandered away from Christ into lifeless formality or heartless skepticism, and heart-sick devotees of worldly pleasure found the abiding joy and peace of the life eternal.

It has been said that the meetings in the Haymarket Theater were in some respects the most remarkable. It is not possible for the writer, by any written description, to convey to a reader anything like an adequate impression of the appearance, the spirit, the movement, the tremendous power and cumulative effect of these meetings. It must suffice to give here the merest shadow sketch of one Sunday's meeting, as a specimen of the whole.

An observer, taking his position in front of the theater at least an hour before the appointed time for opening the doors, found himself not a moment too soon to secure a vantage-place in the gathering crowd. From that time on a constant stream of people came flowing toward the building and massing together before the closed doors. By cable cars, carriages, wagons, carettes, and on foot, from the south side, way out near the Fair grounds, from all parts of the city and from afar, they came, filling the large area, packing and overflowing the sidewalk and the street. The eagerness and intensity of interest manifest in the faces and actions of the multitude was something not soon to be forgotten. As soon as the heavy doors swung open the human waves rolled in, and in a short time all the seats and standing-room on stage, floor, galleries, and boxes were occupied. Three thousand souls were crowded into the building, and it was estimated that from three to four thousand more failed to gain entrance. As soon as the Haymarket was full, packed from stage to dome, another theater, the Standard, three blocks away, was opened to accommodate the overflow. A number of Mr. Moody's workers went about, calling to the disappointed multitude outside the Haymarket, "This way! Overflow meeting at the Standard Theater, three blocks away. This way!" Only a personal explanation and persuasion could induce many to start for the Standard. Some were unwilling to go anywhere except where Mr. Moody appeared in person.

"Can't we get in to get a peep at him?" said one man, who had in his charge several ladies.

"We started here two hours before time," said another, "and we are going to see Mr. Moody if it takes all day."

Soon the Standard Theater also was filled, and still an overflow of hundreds remained to drift away into the

streets again. The parquet, balcony, and gallery presented an unbroken expanse of faces ranged in semicircles
one above another. The stairways were crowded, and on
the stage worshipers sat as closely together as chairs could
be placed. The scenery was drawn up high overhead, and
flies and wings were removed. Every window and door
was thrown open, letting in floods of air and daylight,
and a continuous meeting was held throughout the day,
people going and coming. Some relinquished their places
only long enough to eat luncheon, remaining till 4 P.M.,
when they also were enabled to see and hear Mr. Moody.

The scene in the Haymarket Theater was most striking
and impressive. Looking out from the back of the stage,
which had been cleared of all obstructions, from the footlights to the wall, the eye fell first upon the thousands of
uplifted faces on the floor, then swept upward to the three
great clouds of witnesses in the boxes and galleries that
overhung these, one above another, up to the dizzy height
of the dome. In those endlessly diversified faces turned
toward the stage, where stood the man of God whom all
had come to hear, one could read a varied tale of eager
expectation, anxious desire, carelessness, curiosity, quiet,
confident expectation, painful suspense, spiritual unrest
and struggle, unsatisfied soul-hunger, sorrow and misery,
defiant hardness, gloomy despondency, skeptical indifference, prayerful repose, triumphant faith.

On the stage, massed around and behind Mr. Moody,
were several evangelists and other Christian workers, two
quartets of singers, Towner's male choir, a large body of
male and female singers, and the song leaders, George C.
Stebbins, D. B. Towner, and F. H. Jacobs, with a multitude filling the stage behind them. About four hundred
electric lights cast their glow over the scene.

The opening song-service was conducted with the usual

readiness, promptitude, and tact. Song followed song, from choir, quartet, soloists, and congregation, with prayer in its season, making way for the sermon to follow. It was interesting to see the deepening effect upon the people of the songs, especially the tender, touching solo, "Some Sweet Day," by Mr. Stebbins, and the beautiful, impressive plea by the Towner chorus, "My son, give me thy heart." As these songs were being sung one could see how they won their way into many a heart, stirring them to unwonted thoughts, and opening the fountain of tears.

After the song service Mr. Moody broke in with an announcement. "We want to keep up these meetings," he said. "We go from the Empire Theater because we can no longer get it, and enter the Standard Theater. We want to reach and save the drunkards, the fallen, the wretched, the lost. We want your sympathy and help. Now," he cried, "all who want the theater meetings continued lift up your hands;" and all over the building hands flashed up. "That is very encouraging," continued Mr. Moody. "Now put your hands into your pockets. We are going to take up a collection for the support of the work." This sharp turn amused and pleased the people, for the voters were neatly caught by an immediate test of their sincerity.

After the collection and another song or two, Mr. Moody rose and dashed at once into his subject. He spoke of the triumphant life of the Christian overcomer, the difficulties that beset it, and the glorious rewards that await it in heaven, driving home the word with overpowering unction and effect. "I want to speak about the overcoming life," he said. "Every one is either overcoming or being overcome. I want to tell you how to overcome and who are the overcomers. You and I are more interested in this fight than in any of the great battles of history.

Who is it that overcomes the world? Who is the victor? He that believeth that Jesus is the Son of God.

"When I was converted I thought it was all done, that I could lay the oars in the boat and let the current bear it on. I soon found my mistake. Let none think that the battle is fought when the gift of salvation is received. It is only begun.

"It is folly for any of you to attempt to fight this battle without Christ in you the hope of glory. It is impossible. You must have a new life before you can fight the battle of a Christian life. Abraham, Jacob, Moses, Elijah, Peter, apart from God made wretched failures. They fell at the strongest point of their character. Away from God these strong men were weak as water and were overcome. We stand, we walk, we live, we fight, we overcome by faith.

"It is a good thing to find out who, what, and how strong our enemies are, if we are to fight, and not to underestimate their strength. We have self to overcome. We must overcome it, or be overcome. The greatest enemy that ever crossed my path was D. L. Moody. Our enemies are within. We must get the victory over self, our appetites, passions, lusts. What we want everywhere just now is home piety. Selfishness crucified, and Christlikeness formed. What does it all amount to if you go to church and run all the rounds of a formal Christian life, and live a cold, selfish, unlovely life at home?

"How can I overcome? Treat what you call your weaknesses and infirmities as sins. Confess them to God. Confess to those you have wronged. We must be co-workers with God in this, hate and abhor what he hates, have fellowship with him, then we can overcome in his strength. No enemies can stand before the strength of God, Christ in us. Are you overcoming, or are you being overcome? Have you gained or lost since you began the Christian life?

"One of the most damnable sins of the time is envy, jealousy. It is wide-spread. It eats like a cancer, it burns like fire. God deliver us from it! What we want to-day is a higher type of Christianity. Why don't you say Amen? [Cries of "Amen!"] We are a bad lot! We may as well know it! Begin now and set yourself right with God. Get victory over yourself. Begin there, at home. Get the overcoming power. Stand for God. Dare to do right! Dare to be right! Dare to stand alone!

"Look at the eight 'overcomes' of Revelation. Look at the exceeding great rewards of those who overcome. It is wonderful. Oh, the riches of grace and glory! It is said of certain New York millionaires that their fortunes are so large they can't tell how rich they are. That's my case! I am a millionaire! You didn't know it, did you? Well, I am! I can't tell how rich I am. He that overcometh shall inherit all things, *all things*, ALL THINGS! Think of that! 'All things are yours!'"

The people were profoundly impressed by the truth, and many expressed a desire to be saved. These were invited to the front, where a number of Christian workers met them for conversation, and put into their hands copies of Mr. Moody's book, "The Way and the Word," showing the way of life to the inquiring soul. With prayer and song the service closed, and the assembled thousands, from all parts of the land, dispersed to meet never again in this world.

CHAPTER XV.

WE have witnessed a specimen Sunday service in the Haymarket Theater, conducted by Mr. Moody. Now we go to a Monday evening meeting in the Empire Theater. We go out West Madison Street. On our way we pass all kinds of places whereunto men and women repair to seek amusement, to kill time, to inflame passion, to feed lust, to breed crime. What sights and sounds and smells are here! What swarms of poor, degraded, wretched, ruined beings are here, seeking again the fire that has scorched and blistered them, body and soul; handling again the biting serpent and stinging adder; crawling deeper and deeper into viler fellowships and more damning pollutions.

We pause in the blaze of the electric light at the opening of the theater. A stream of all sorts of people is flowing through its wide, marble-paved hall, into auditorium, boxes, and galleries. We enter. There is no scenery on the stage. The footlights are out. The company of men and women clustered together there are not in stage dress. No artificial, imitation human beings are they, to stand as counterfeits of the mighty or the ignoble dead. Only a company of twoscore Christian singers, with a gospel preacher or two, servants of Jesus Christ, come to bear witness on that stage to the most stupendous facts and realities ever disclosed in this world of shadow and sham.

82

Just now a burst of song silences the hum of voices and the stir of restless feet. Beside the organ on the stage stands the gospel singer, Mr. D. B. Towner, pouring forth a stream of rich melody that swells to the roof and rolls out into the crowded street. Every word of the song rings out with enunciation so clear and distinct, and withal so richly musical and true, that he who runs may hear and understand and enjoy. The people stop on the street to listen, and come in to hear more. Song after song follows —solo, duet, quartet, chorus, congregational, intermingled with brief prayers that go straight to the mark. And still the people are coming, some to stand awhile on the rim of the auditorium, to see what it all means, then drift away again to more congenial associations, others to stay for what is to follow.

The conductor of this strange "performance" is Rev. R. A. Torrey, superintendent of the Chicago Bible Institute. He drives through the service with Moody-like energy, losing not a moment nor an opportunity. He rises to preach and leaps right into his subject, rushing on with increasing momentum of thought and energy, gripping the reason and conscience of his hearers with the divine logic of the Word of God, and bearing them along to his inevitable conclusion. His theme is Repentance. Yes, repentance on the stage, in the theater. It is needed there. Ah, this is more than a play. The "scenery" is visible only to the soul. Its background is the judgment-throne of God, and the white light of eternity plays over the whole scene. The "actors" are not on the stage to-night, but in the boxes and the seats of the auditorium and galleries—sinful men and women face to face with the truth and Spirit of God, deciding questions of life and death for time and eternity.

The preacher drives home the declaration of Acts xvii.

30, that "God now commandeth all men everywhere to repent." He shows that John the Baptist and Christ and the apostles, Paul included, preached repentance, and that the prophets of the Old Testament preached practically the same truth, and concludes that a subject that occupied so much of the attention of the inspired preachers must be of great importance. He defines repentance as simply a change of mind which issues in a change of conduct. The sinner must change his mind about sin, about God, and about Christ, accepting the Bible view in place of his own, turning away from sin, turning to God to obey him and to Christ to accept him. "Anybody in this theater now can repent here and now. He cannot do it without the Spirit of God, but the Spirit is trying now to bring you to repentance, and you can now repent."

Why should you repent? First, because God commands it. He "now commandeth all men everywhere to repent." Second, unless you do you shall perish. That man there, that woman in the gallery, good or bad, must repent or perish. Third, because you must appear before the judgment-seat of Christ. You adulterer, you robber, you swindler, you seducer, you Sabbath-breaker, you blasphemer, you rejecter of Jesus Christ, must appear before the judgment of God! Fourth, because repentance brings pardon. When one truly repents God will blot out all his sins. Oh, you robber, you murderer, you drunkard, repent and turn to God and he will blot out all your sins. Thank God for a gospel that wipes out forever all sins of the sad past! Fifth, because God is love. "The goodness of God leadeth thee to repentance." The preacher presses the truth upon the conscience with great power, with manifest effect.

The faces of the listening people are a study. They make unconscious revelations of what is going on within as the Spirit of God applies the truth to their hearts. Near the stage we see a strong, square, firm face that is darkening with unutterable woe. It makes one shudder. There is one over whose gloom we see the light of a new resolve slowly come to its rising. There is one whose pitiful soul-hunger moves to tears. There is another racked by conflicting emotions that betray the struggle of a convicted soul. Not a few tell the tale of awful depravity, almost hopeless hardening, seared consciences, determined hatred and resistance of the truth. But, thank God, a number of convicted ones yield to the better impulse to repent and turn to God.

The sermon closes with a prayer, then Mr. Towner pleads tenderly in song, " Will you not come to Him now ? " Another hymn follows, another prayer, than an after-meeting, when a number of persons arise at the call of the preacher in token of their desire for salvation. A touching duet follows, while Christians silently pray, then a closing prayer for the repentant ones, and another season of song, while the preacher and other Christians pass to and fro among the people to deal with individual souls about their salvation. With this the meeting ends, but some still linger to a late hour, held by the pleading of some loving heart.

CHAPTER XVI.

FROM EMPIRE TO STANDARD THEATER.

THE second theater which Mr. Moody succeeded in entering with the gospel was the Empire, not far from the Haymarket. For five weeks, every evening, and thrice on Sundays, the building was made to ring with song, prayer, sermon, and testimony. In this, as in the other places of similar character, the masses of the people were found accessible to a remarkable degree. The work was greatly blessed. Many striking cases of conversion came to the knowledge of the workers during those meetings. Strangers from afar, men caught in the rapids of dissipation, and tossed about in saloons, gambling-dens, and other vile resorts, miserable prodigals far and long from home, despairing wretches on the verge of hell, drifted into the theater meetings and there heard the sweet gospel story, and found salvation from sin and death.

After five weeks the owner of the Empire Theater declined to extend the lease to the evangelists. The closing meeting was held on Saturday evening, August 19th, conducted by Evangelist Merton Smith. A special effort was made to reach the intemperate with songs, testimonies, sermon, and appeal. The Scotch evangelist, Rev. John McNeill, delivered the principal address. He was in his happiest mood and at his best, playing at will on the responsive heart-chords of the multitude before him. He gave a fascinating bit of autobiography, in language, spirit, style, and manner simply inimitable. With a few sim-

ple master-touches he set before our often tear-dimmed
eyes an exquisite picture of the home of his childhood,
one of those typical Scottish homes which are the seed-
beds of all manly virtues and womanly graces, the glory
of the better Scotland whose magnificent contribution to
the world has been a galaxy of godly heroes that shine as
the stars forever and ever. As he spoke of the cheery,
happy home life, the strong, noble, godly father, and the
sweet, gentle mother, and turned it all into an overwhelming plea for happy homes, many a face was wet with tears
and lighted up with new resolve for the better life. Re-
peating Burns's "Cotter's Saturday Night," he said that
what the poet pictured was a reality under his father's
roof. When the scene stood complete before us, the
speaker broke into a tender, touching appeal that went
irresistibly to the heart. "Come back to your father's
God!" he cried. The people were profoundly moved, and
in many cases emotion ripened into holy resolve and resolute decision for Christ. The simple story of his own
conversion at a railroad-station deepened the impression
as this unreportable address drew to its close.

The next day, Sunday, the meetings were transferred
from the Empire to the Standard Theater, a building capable of accommodating about 2500 persons, located in one
of the darkest spots in Chicago, in a solid block of vile
resorts, where abominable iniquity ran riot to the damna-
tion of multitudes.

The first service in the new place proved the wisdom of
the choice. The house was packed, and hundreds had to
go away disappointed. Rev. Dr. C. I. Scofield, of Dallas,
Tex., preached with power. Another meeting followed at
4 P.M., addressed by Mr. Moody and Major Whittle, with
service of song by Towner, Stebbins, Jacobs, Atkinson,
and the Kimball Quartet. So great was the desire of

many strangers to hear Mr. Moody that they remained over from the morning service in order to secure places in the crowded building, from which so many had to go away disappointed. A third meeting was held in the evening, addressed by Rev. R. A. Torrey. In all these meetings the influence of the Holy Spirit rested manifestly upon the people, and it seemed as if a visible divine seal were being stamped upon the enterprise.

Evening after evening during this opening week the work continued with a deepening sense of God's presence in the meetings. One evening, after a sermon of convicting power by Mr. Torrey, while the preacher was pointing many inquirers in the auditorium to Christ, Mr. Towner, the song leader, was doing the same thing on the stage, where a number were converted. On another evening, after addresses by Colonel Hadley, the well-known mission worker of New York City, and Mr. Torrey, about three fourths of the congregation remained for the inquiry-meeting, and many came into the light of a new life.

On Thursday evening Mr. Moody spoke on the loving tenderness of Christ with divine power. Himself most deeply moved by the truth he preached, his tears fell like rain and his voice choked and thrilled with emotion, as his yearning heart went out toward the poor lost souls for whom Jesus died. The power of God came upon the people. All over the house were faces wet with tears, and hard hearts melted like wax at the presence of the Lord in the tenderness of his love. The promise of the opening week was amply fulfilled in the weeks that followed, for the meetings in the Standard Theater, from that time to the close of the campaign, were among the most successful held anywhere. From two to four times every Sunday, and every evening of the week, the gospel was preached with saving effect to multitudes of people, many of them the worst and most wretched of their kind.

CHAPTER XVII.

GOOD CHEER—PROGRESS—OBJECT-LESSON.

It is well known to all who are acquainted with Mr. Moody that he is a Christian optimist, or, rather, a man of luminous faith, cheery hope, intrepid courage, and unquenchable enthusiasm. He has learned the beautiful Pauline lesson of "forgetting those things that are behind, and reaching forth unto those things which are before." He believes that in order to succeed in Christian work the workers must be "of good courage." All this was most manifest in the most trying times of the campaign. Always looking on the bright side—that is, the God side—of things, he not only inspired others with his own contagious faith and courage, but took every opportunity to encourage, cheer, and spur them on by word and deed. To his clear view the successive days grew better and better, even when some of his friends failed to discern the signs as he did. "I believe this is the best day Chicago has ever seen," said he, again and again. And he knew the Chicago he spoke about. "Before the World's Fair closes," he confidently declared, "we shall have great blessing." He had an assurance that could not fail. "Think," said he, as his glance swept over the thousands of eager faces that looked into his, "think of the people from these meetings carrying the sacred fire with them into all the places where they go, throughout this country and in other lands! Never have I seen such eagerness to hear the gospel of Jesus Christ as in these days. I think I have not seen in America anything that has been more encouraging than the work in Chicago in the last three months."

"I believe," he said, on another occasion, "that we shall see signs and wonders in these days. It seems as if there is a wave of salvation about to flow over this land. It seems to me that the country is ripe for one of the greatest religious awakenings it has ever seen. In our great prosperity many of us have forgotten God, and the present time of business depression, disappointment, and suffering is bringing men to realize their need of Jesus Christ. I am looking for a great movement throughout the country the coming fall and winter. If the Church of God would only wake up, we should certainly have the greatest revival the world has ever known. We are surely going to win this battle if we hold on long enough. Let us see to it that we ourselves are quickened and filled with the Spirit, that we may be ready for our God-given opportunity to do our part in the great work."

Again he said: "The year 1890 was a good year, but 1891 was better, 1892 better still, and 1893 best of all, and if I live to see 1894 I expect that year will be better than 1893. 'The path of the just is as the shining light, that shineth more and more unto the perfect day.' I believe we are living in the grandest days this century or this age has seen. Some one in Chicago recently said that the Sabbath is a pest, and must be wiped out. Instead of the Sabbath being wiped out, I don't know but God is going to turn all the week-days into holy Sabbaths, and give us days of heaven on this earth." It was with this trustful, hopeful, cheery, fore-looking spirit that the great and difficult enterprise in Chicago was commenced, continued, and completed.

At the beginning of the fourth month, August, the evangelistic forces occupied about ten churches, seven halls, two theaters, and five tents, the latter being moved from one strategic point to another, as occasion required. Up to this time the north, the west, and the south sides of the wide-spreading city, with its suburbs, were reached with a succession of attractive, powerful, and effective meetings. From two to three hundred workers were in active service, under the capable leadership of the experienced lieutenants whom Mr. Moody had called to his aid. At this time an aggregate of about 120 gospel meetings, exclusive of many gatherings for prayer and counsel, were held weekly, fifteen on week-days, and from twenty-five to thirty on Sundays. From 30,000 to 40,000 persons came under the influence of the gospel on Sunday. On several occasions all-day meetings were held in the tents, with attendance and sustained interest that were simply amazing. It seemed almost incredible that two great theaters on the same street, nearly opposite each other, should be filled to hear the gospel, while some 500 more people tried in vain to enter.

The last Sunday in August surpassed all preceding days in the extent of the work done. About sixty-five meetings were held, in thirty-five different places throughout the city and suburbs, including fifteen churches, two theaters, five halls, five tents, and in the open air, with the gospel wagon, and elsewhere. About thirty-six ministers, evangelists, and song leaders, with from two to three hundred other Christian workers from the Bible Institute and elsewhere, officiated. An aggregate of over 51,000 people heard the gospel in these various meetings, many of whom were brought to a knowledge of the truth and acceptance of Christ as their Saviour. In the face of the fears that had been entertained of a decrease of interest and consequent falling off in attendance during the month of August, this triumphant record was especially cheering.

This Sunday also marked the close of a ten days' session of the International Conference of the Christian and Missionary Alliance, which, under the presidency of Rev. A. B. Simpson, of New York, had been held in the Chicago Avenue Church. The conference was more or less interlinked with the plan and movement of the evangelistic campaign. Its morning sessions were devoted exclusively to Bible study. From nine to twelve each day large audiences occupied the church to listen to such eminent Bible teachers as Dr. Scofield of Texas, Dr. Chapell of Boston, Dr. Oerter of New York, and Dr. Stearns of Philadelphia. The afternoons and evenings were occupied by addresses on such themes as Practical Holiness, Divine Healing, and the Evangelization of the World. Devotional meetings occupied the intervals, morning, noon, and night, between the main services, and contributed largely to keeping the interest of the meetings at white heat. The Alliance has between 200 and 300 missionaries in the foreign field, and hopes to send many more abroad during the coming years, having important stations in China, India, and Africa. Many returned missionaries were in attendance at the convention, and gave frequent addresses on the different phases of their work.

The two daily Bible lectures in the Bible Institute had been continued up to this time with increasing interest, and some of the most eminent Bible teachers and preachers of Europe and America were there heard with great delight and profit by thousands of Bible students from all parts of the world. After the close of the Alliance Conference, in order to secure more room and to make the service more popular in character, the lectures were transferred to the large auditorium of the Chicago Avenue

Church. There for one week the lectures were delivered to larger congregations, the services being diversified in various ways by Mr. Moody. Himself being one of the lecturers, he sometimes displaced himself by calling upon other ministers to open the word in his stead. On three successive days he invited several of the recently arrived speakers to introduce themselves in short addresses, and also to give specimens of Scotch and English expository preaching, which was greatly enjoyed.

The day preceding the close of the Alliance Conference, the last hour of the forenoon was set apart on the program for a lecture on the Bible by Mr. Moody. This afforded him a double opportunity to hold up and magnify the Word of God, and at the same time give a most inspiring and impressive object-lesson on the elements of successful evangelism. It was the only one of the scores of services on the program of the conference which was thoroughly advertised and for which special efforts were made by circulation of tickets, after the approved fashion of the Moody evangelistic meetings. The result was a revelation to many, when they found that even at such an hour as eleven o'clock on Saturday, the big church rapidly filled up till auditorium and galleries were occupied.

There was another revelation when the meeting opened in Mr. Moody's characteristic way, with his prompt, swift, electrifying movement, sweeping through a song service of about twenty-five minutes that roused, thrilled, and kindled all hearts, in preparation for the discourse that was to follow. It was glorious, and full of the spirit of devotion. In this devotional service four songs were sung by the congregation, led by a well-trained, powerful chorus choir, with instrumental accompaniment; two beautiful solos, by ladies, in the chorus of one of them the great congregation and choir joining with thrilling

power; three impressive and affecting songs by quartets,
two male, one female; and one magnificent hymn by a
strong male choir.   Three prayers were intermingled with
the music.   The service was so arranged and ordered that
it had the effect of an upward movement, like the swell
of a wave, carrying the worshipers away from their dis-
tracting thoughts into the waiting-place of devotion, with
minds and hearts opened to the word that was to follow.

When the entire service of seventy-five minutes came
to its close, embracing ten songs, five prayers, a lecture
on the Bible by Mr. Moody, full of fire and energy, and
concluding remarks by Dr. A. B. Simpson, that fell like
heavenly dew upon the hearts of the audience, it seemed
as if but half the time had passed.

After the opening song service Mr. Moody remarked
that some of his hearers had doubtless been wondering
why they had so much singing before the preaching began.
"We had so much singing here this morning," said he,
"to show you how a live, spirited, attractive gospel service can be made.   There is no excuse for dull, spiritless,
unattractive gospel meetings.   It is a mistake to regard
the sermon as the only important thing in a meeting, or
even as the main thing.   There is often more gospel in
such songs as we sing than in the sermon.   The song
may carry the gospel into many hearts that the sermon
does not reach.   And it prepares the people for the sermon. . Wake up! Wake up the people! Get them out
to your meetings.   Advertise your meetings.   Let the people know about it.   Compel them to come.   Press things.
Why preach to a few when you might have hundreds ?
Why have poor, dull, sleepy meetings when you might
have them full of life, enthusiasm, and power? If we
believe the gospel is the best news that ever came to this
world, then let us publish it to everybody we can reach."

CHAPTER XVIII.

A NEW DEPARTURE.

AFTER careful consideration of the hazard and the expense involved, an important new departure was taken, by securing the use of the Central Music Hall for daily meetings, during the last two months of the campaign. It was arranged to hold one or two services each Sunday and a two hours' service each week-day, from 11 A.M. to 1 P.M., with Mr. Moody and Mr. McNeill as the principal speakers. The building was admirably located and adapted for the purpose, its central place in the business portion making it the best strategic point in the city for a continuous gospel work. There were some to whom it seemed an ill-considered movement, and at least a very questionable and hazardous experiment to push into the very business heart of the city, to solicit a hearing for the gospel of Christ in the midday hours of the busy days. But faith takes not counsel of human fears or improbabilities. A glad surprise awaited the doubting ones, and the wisdom of the choice was demonstrated in the first service.

The opening meeting in the new place was assigned to Rev. John McNeill on the morning of the first Sunday in September. After a delightful service of song and prayer the preacher poured out his heart in a sermon of wonderful beauty and grace, that held the vast audience in gladsome captivity of mind and heart to the close. There was no more question as to the feasibility of Sunday meetings in the Music Hall. The preacher had won his audience and assured himself a welcome and a hearing from that day forth.

At 4 P.M. of the same day a meeting of special interest was to take place. Mr. Moody had sent repeated and urgent invitations to the Rev. Dr. Adolf Stoecker, ex-court preacher of Germany, to join his forces in a special effort in behalf of the German people of Chicago, and now the famous German was expected to make his first appearance on the American platform. The announcement caused considerable excitement, as well as genuine interest, and the Hall was filled to overflowing with an immense audience of the flower of Chicago's German population, including a large number of ministers and representative Christian workers.

But a disappointment was in store for the congregation, and not less so for Mr. Moody, who had charge of the meeting, for the expected speaker had been delayed on the way hither, and could not reach the city in time for the appointment. Mr. Moody explained the embarrassing situation as best he could, declining to respond to the call of the audience to preach himself, and called upon Rev. Niclaus Boldt, a young German evangelist of St. Paul, who preached a short, timely sermon.

As it was known that some of the daily papers had indulged in ungracious criticism of Mr. Moody for having invited Dr. Stoecker to Chicago, utterly misrepresenting the object of the German preacher's mission, and as there were some misgivings in the minds of many who were concerned for the success of the evangelistic work, Mr. Moody took occasion to state his reasons for his action. " I will tell you," said he, " why I tried to get Dr. Stoecker here. Because he is a man of God who is giving his life

for the welfare of the people, and has been greatly used
of God. He is trying to do in Germany just what I am
trying to do here—to reach the non-church-going masses
with the gospel of Christ for their salvation. He has
institutions in Berlin somewhat like our Bible Institute
here, and is doing the same work. I have great respect
for a man who comes out of the royal court to do the
work that he does. He is a man after my own heart. I
want him here to speak the word of life to his own fellow-
countrymen in this great city."

These timely words, nobly spoken, had their effect, showing at once the unselfish, generous motive that prompted
Mr. Moody's call of Dr. Stoecker, and his unshaken confidence in and high esteem for the man.

The third meeting of the day was held in the Hall in
the evening. At an early hour the place was crowded,
hundreds were turned away, and still they continued to
come and go until near the close of the service. Mr.
Moody preached the sermon, his theme being his favorite
Daniel, which always kindles the speaker's soul and sets
the souls of the hearers aflame.

On Monday many a Christian worker went to the Music
Hall with serious misgivings, to see the outcome of the
first experiment of a two hours' midday meeting. The
day seemed an especially unfavorable one for the beginning. in that place. It was Labor Day, the streets were
thronged with great processions, and the air was filled with
a tumult of sound, musical and otherwise; yet the large
hall was filled, and the two hours of the meeting were
made glorious with song and sermon and prayer. The
whole service seemed like a mighty burst of inspiration.
The power of God came down upon the people. An unseen hand seemed to guide the meeting from first to last.
Song after song rolled forth with the musical waves of

the big organ, and prayer after prayer rose up to God like sweet incense of hearts aglow with love divine. Mr. Moody prayed especially that the last two months of the meetings might be the most blessed and fruitful of all, and memorable to all eternity in the experience of many. He cried to God with tender pleading for Heaven's greatest blessing on the preachers who had lately arrived, and on those who had already so faithfully labored and borne the heat and burden of the summer's work.

Before proceeding with the service, Mr. Moody made some statements with reference to the new departure, saying, among other things: "We have been working for four months in various parts of the city, and now we have secured this Central Music Hall for two months, to reach the business center with the gospel in the middle of the day. We have got the help of a number of eminent ministers from home and abroad. We want a little Scotch fire here, a little English fire, and a little German fire. We have distinguished speakers to speak to us every day. These meetings will accommodate the many World's Fair visitors, and the business men in this central part of the city who are anxious to hear these men of God. Many who come here to listen to the word of life will be quickened and renewed, as they go away from here into all parts of the land and the world, and they will carry this fire to their own towns, churches, and homes, and set them on fire for God. That is what we want, that is what we are praying and laboring for."

The London evangelist, Henry Varley, being called upon, arose to speak, but he had hardly begun to open his subject when the delayed German guest, Dr. Stoecker, entered the Hall. Mr. Moody arose, exclaiming, "Let us receive the court preacher of Germany," and the people stood up to welcome him with hand-clapping and happy

smiles. Then Mr. Varley proceeded with his discourse,
setting forth the glorious Lord Jesus Christ as "God's
center of gravity," pleading with commanding power for
the recognition and acknowledgment of the Lord as the
center of the individual life, of the family, of the home,
of the city, of the nation, of the world. The sermon was
a triumph of sacred oratory, bearing the vast audience
along as on the crest of a mighty wave.

The sermon ended, the congregation poured out their
hearts in the exulting words and strains of the majestic
old hymn,

> How firm a foundation, ye saints of the Lord,
> Is laid for your faith in his excellent Word.

Then short addresses were made by Rev. John Robertson,
of Glasgow, and Dr. H. M. Wharton, of Baltimore, Md.,
holding forth Jesus as the only Saviour and hope of men,
and commending the old gospel of the grace of God in all
simplicity and truth.

After more song and prayer, with special supplication
in behalf of Dr. Stoecker, Mr. Moody introduced his honored guest, who made a very judicious and pertinent introductory address, which was interpreted for English ears
by Rev. Niclaus Boldt. He expressed his appreciation of
the kind reception given him. He disclaimed the motives and purposes which hostile papers had attributed to
him in coming to America. "I came not to attack the
Jews," he said, with a fine thrill of indignant feeling. "I
came to preach the Word of God to my German brethren.
I came not to see America or the World's Fair, but to
take part with dear Mr. Moody in his work of evangelization in your great city. I had a desire to come before,
but as court preacher I was under orders, and could not
come. Now I am no more court preacher of the German

Empire. I am a preacher of the people. I am no longer under orders, but free to come and go. It is in my heart to testify of my glorious God to the thousands of my countrymen who are here, and who will come from all points of the compass to visit the World's Fair. I would bring them a message of tender remembrance and love from their brethren in the old fatherland. I would strengthen their love and loyalty to the new fatherland they have found. And I would constrain them by the love of Christ to seek a home in the everlasting fatherland above, where our loved departed ones abide.

"Our generation has come upon one of the great crises of world-history. This is felt everywhere, in the intellectual, the spiritual, and the physical realms. This is preeminently the time of separation, of judgment, of decision. The wheat and the tares must be revealed. The beginning of the end is at hand, when the kingdom of God and the world will meet in the awful collision of the final battle. In the great conflict of the present crisis Germany seems to feel the shock first. There the forces are marshaling and massing for the onset. As the clouds are gathering fast and ominously over our dear old fatherland, we look up to God for help, and we pray that he will not forsake his people in the land of the Reformation. Brethren, I implore you all who bear the name of our blessed Master, do not suffer your eyes to be blinded and your hearts deceived by the worldly riches and glory of material progress and prosperity. The things which are seen are temporal; the things which are not seen are eternal and abiding. In the great conflict let us take sides with our God, and stand for truth and right, for the welfare of man and the honor of Christ."

At the conclusion of Dr. Stoecker's address Mr. Moody arose with a glowing face, and exclaimed: "I thank God for this day. I thank God for the coming of this dear man of God. We don't regard the papers that speak against him. I am exceedingly gratified to note that nearly every German church here has been thrown open to him. I don't know of any man in Christendom that I would rather have stand in the pulpit of our church than this dear brother." Then, turning to Dr. Stoecker, Mr. Moody continued: "We give you a warm welcome! God bless you! We don't believe the newspapers. We believe the Bible. We have confidence in you. We love you!"

A brief address by Mr. McNeill, witty and wise, closed this remarkable initiatory meeting of the midday series. There remained no doubt of the wisdom of the new departure. It was a fair beginning, with promise of better things yet to come, whereof all were glad in the anticipation of faith. It was a striking object-lesson set before the eyes of the hurrying thousands on business and pleasure bent—two hours out of the heart of each day devoted to the consideration of things unseen and eternal, while the foaming waves of worldly traffic beat upon the walls within which the worshipers waited upon the Lord. It was a daily standing protest against the mammon worship of the busy mart, and an appeal to the unsatisfied cravings of the soul that cannot live by bread alone.

CHAPTER XIX.

THE occupancy of the Central Music Hall for daily meetings was not the only advance step taken at the beginning of the fifth month, although perhaps the most important. The fair promise of the opening days in that place was more than fulfilled during the first week, in the surprisingly large, constant attendance of World's Fair visitors, business people, and others, and the increasing and deepening interest in the services. Two days of the first week were especially memorable on account of the overwhelming power of the Word of God and the awfully solemn sense of the reality and presence of the unseen and the eternal.

The principal addresses of the days were given by Mr. Moody and Mr. McNeill, supplemented by Drs. J. W. Chapman, H. M. Wharton, and John Riddell, Revs. John Robertson and A. C. Dixon, and Evangelist Henry Varley. The service of song was given a prominent place, represented by such singers as Sankey, Stebbins, Towner, Burke, Jacobs, Atkinson, the Princeton and the Ladies' Institute Quartets, and a strong chorus choir.

Among the principal new places secured as centers of operation at this time were two theaters, in addition to the three already in use, namely, the Columbia and the Windsor, in the heart of the city. At the South Park M. E. Church about twenty different churches were united for a grand, combined effort, under the leadership of Dr. H. M. Wharton and the singer, George C. Stebbins. The Third Presbyterian Church united with a half-dozen other churches for a forward movement, with Dr. J. W. Chapman in charge. The first service in the Columbia Theater was in the hands of Rev. John McNeill and his singing companion, Mr. Burke. In the Windsor Theater Major Whittle and F. Schiverea conducted the first meeting. Ira D. Sankey, who had just returned from Northfield, sang the gospel at not less than eight different meetings during the Sunday. Rev. A. C. Dixon, fresh, vigorous, and strong, preached five times during the day, in the Model Sunday-school Building and the Epworth Tabernacle, at the Fair grounds, where the congregations consisted of World's Fair visitors, of whom hundreds were ministers of the gospel, teachers, and students. D. B. Towner conducted the service of song in all these meetings.

The work in the five tabernacle tents reached perhaps its highest point of interest and success during the fifth month. Many thousands of people, of whom large numbers were strangers to church services, there heard the gospel from the lips of some of the best people's preachers in the land. Evangelist Schiverea tried the experiment of holding two successive all-day meetings in his big tent, embracing sixteen different services, beginning at 9 A.M. and closing at about 10 P.M. These were remarkable meetings, blazing with enthusiasm, full of power, and marked with glorious results. Prayer, praise, and song filled the intervals of the addresses. The speakers who preached the Word during the two days were, in their order, Dr. John Riddell, Rev. A. C. Dixon, Evangelist Schiverea, Rev. John McNeill, Dr. H. M. Wharton, Merton Smith, Henry Varley, J. H. Elliott, Rev. Dr. Stoecker, and Rev. John Robertson. Two children's meetings were conducted by Major D. W. Whittle and Miss B. B. Tyson. The singing force consisted of Messrs. Stebbins, Burke, Jacobs, Atkinson, and the Kimball, Oberlin, Institute, and Ladies' Quartets.

At the Bible Institute the daily morning lectures were delivered by Dr. John Riddell, and multitudes of visitors continued to share with the students the invaluable opportunity of searching the Scriptures under such masterly teaching. Mr. Moody, in addition to the burden of the management and his daily sermons at Central Music Hall, also preached and labored in various churches during the week evenings, including in the number one of the Bohemian churches. Dr. Stoecker preached a series of week-night sermons in the Chicago Avenue Church, to which were invited the German people of the city. He concluded the week's teaching by taking his hearers into the Book of Revelation for a look into eternity and a view of the millennial age of the world, when the socialistic dream of an earthly paradise shall be realized, not in the wisdom, power, and achievements of man, but in the grace and power of God. The series of sermons culminating in this were admirable for their simplicity, clearness, scripturalness, adaptation, and heart-warming application. They made a most wholesome and beneficent impression on the scores of ministers and thousands of people who heard them.

The first announced appearance of Dr. Stoecker, on Sunday afternoon, before an immense multitude of representative German people in Central Music Hall, was an important and critical occasion for the speaker and for the cause he represented. Deeply realizing this, the preacher came up to it with the calm confidence and trained powers for which he is so remarkable, and in the name of his Lord he turned the opportunity into a sublime triumph.

It was a scene and an experience seldom repeated. The orator was at his best—alert, keen, aglow with intellectual and spiritual ardor, enkindling thought, and restrained emotion. His discourse was a masterpiece of sacred oratory, from a preacher greater than his sermon, and the effect was profound and overwhelming.

The meetings of this month were characterized by a widening scope, increased working forces, more thorough organization, and more manifest results. But perhaps the most remarkable, and certainly the most striking and gratifying, feature of the whole movement was the almost incredible extent of its constituency as it became manifest week by week. Tributary streams of sympathy and aid came flowing into that great reservoir from every part of our land and other lands beyond the seas. Living nerves of close connection between that center of prayer and effort and millions of praying people constituted a prayer union in evangelistic labors the like of which has never before been known. Thousands of churches, Christian Associations, Endeavor Societies, Sunday-schools, and other Christian organizations were constantly being drawn into the mighty fellowship of the movement. The results of blessing coming from such a world-wide fellowship of sympathy, prayer, and effort are simply incalculable.

Gratifying reports from near and from far-away places brought cheering testimony to Mr. Moody and his associates, assuring them of rich blessings received from the evangelistic meetings. Souls newly revived and fired with godly zeal for the work of Christ's kingdom had gone away from the Chicago meetings to their homes and churches to take up neglected duties and to stand forth as living witnesses for the Christ whom they had dishonored by silence and neglect. Thus already had it come to pass, as Mr. Moody hoped and prayed, that souls there converted and Christians quickened, "from all parts of the world, were carrying the fire back with them to their homes."

Mr. Moody had repeatedly heard it said that the World's Fair visitors were not reached by his meetings to any great extent. Accordingly he put the matter to a decisive test on several occasions, as did also some of his workers, with surprising results. It was found, for instance, that of a congregation of about 3000 in the Haymarket Theater, all save about 200 were visitors! A similar test in one of the largest churches showed that about 1900 out of a congregation of 2000 were World's Fair visitors. Further tests by Dr. Munhall, Dr. Dixon, and others revealed the astounding fact that nearly every State of the Union was represented in the congregations, as well as lands beyond the sea.

Sunday, September 17th, was a memorable day of the campaign. On the evening of that day, as the evangelists, one by one, came into the headquarters office at the Bible Institute, and with shining faces reported the work of the day, Mr. Moody broke out with thanksgiving. "Thank God! thank God!" He said it was the best day of all the four and a half months' campaign, and the best Sunday he had experienced in Chicago. "It was a day of great grace and blessing. There was more melting divine power in every one of my meetings than ever before. The people just melted down under the power of God." Others spoke of unusual blessing in their meetings, the constraining power of the gospel, the deeply affected congregations, the many decisions of penitent hearts for Christ. As usual, in some of the places the overflow of people was great enough to have filled other large halls with hungry-hearted hearers. Not less than sixty-four different meetings were held during the day, with a carefully estimated aggregate attendance of from 62,000 to 64,000 hearers, which is about 10,000 more than any previous Sunday. Among the places occupied during the day were nine churches, five tents, five theaters, six halls, various mission-houses, and a number of places in the open air where the gospel wagon gathered the drifting crowds together. Well might the company of evangelists at the close of such a day of blessing fall upon their knees together, while Mr. Moody poured out his soul with them in thanksgiving and praise to the Lord for his grace and goodness.

CHAPTER XX.

THE midday meetings in the Central Music Hall continued to be a daily joy and triumph. No more powerful, impressive, and effective meetings were held during the entire campaign. Every day the speakers seemed to have given them just the word for the hour, as no program or prearrangement could possibly have brought it to pass.

For three days the meetings were transferred to the Columbia Theater, without decreasing the attendance or abating the interest. Mr. Moody, in conducting these daily meetings, called upon various speakers for short addresses, in addition to his own and those of Rev. John McNeill, who spoke every day. Among the additional speakers were Mr. Henry Varley, Rev. John Robertson, Drs. Dixon, Wharton, Riddell, and Chapman, and Major Whittle. The short, spirited, pointed addresses thus delivered were models of evangelistic preaching. During ten consecutive days Mr. Moody spoke on the subject of prayer, presenting one of ten elements of prayer each day, and recapitulating and newly enforcing the points already presented.

One of the meetings which seemed especially marked by its spiritual warmth and moving, melting power was that of Saturday, September 16th. Mr. Moody was the first speaker. His heart was almost too full for utterance. The burden of souls was heavy upon him. The despairing cry of Chicago's perishing thousands was in his ears. He spoke with a passionate yearning for the salvation of the lost, and an almost uncontrollable emotion that bowed all hearts into tearful sympathy with the burning utterances of the speaker. He began by reading from the Book of Daniel the words: "They that be wise shall shine as the brightness of the firmament; and they that turn many to righteousness, as the stars forever and ever." After picturing with a few graphic touches the godly old statesman to whom the angel spoke the quoted words, and pointing to the exceeding rewards of service in soul-saving, the speaker said:

"I have taken this theme to-day to encourage us to take hold of the great work that lies at our hands in this city in these wonderful days. I thank God that I am living in this day and in Chicago. The opportunity of a lifetime is before us to do a work for God that shall make all heaven to sing for joy.

"Let us not spend time splitting hairs in theology and wrangling about creeds. Let us go to work and save lost souls. Our gospel is the only hope of the drunkard, the gambler, the harlot, the outcast, the despairing, the lost on the streets of Chicago. Oh, let us go and save them! Let us stretch out our hands and keep them from rushing into the pit! All over this city are souls just hungry to hear the gospel of hope, just waiting for a loving Christian heart to lay hold on them. Mr. Varley tells us that during the week about five hundred men have been blessed in the Standard Theater meetings. I would rather save one soul from death than have a monument of solid gold reaching from my grave to the heavens! I tell you the monument I want after I am dead and gone is a monument with two legs going about the world—a saved sinner telling of the salvation of Jesus Christ.

"I don't know that I have ever seen a time in Chicago for over thirty years when men seemed to be as ready to be talked to about their souls. Talk to them! Tell them of Jesus, who can save them from their sins and wretchedness! Tell them on the streets, in the cars, in their homes, in the meetings! Speak a word of hope and help and life to those poor, hungry hearts! I believe more can be done in this city during the next six weeks than at any time before, if we all go to work and keep at it. It is our harvest time. It is the day of the Lord. It is the accepted time."

Certainly no more successful soul-saving work was ever done in Chicago than that in the theaters, halls, and tents. It was simply astonishing how the "lapsed masses" and the "lost masses" could be laid hold of in those places. Many a poor castaway was there brought to the refuge and peace of God.

The number of meetings held on the last Sunday of September exceeded the highest record yet made, numbering seventy-five. Recent additions to his working force, such as George C. Needham, Major-General Howard, Charles Inglis, Lord Bennett, and Lord Kinnaird, enabled Mr. Moody to extend the scope of the work. Although so large a number of places were occupied by the evangelists, the demand was still greater than the supply, and a number of open doors waited in vain to receive invited workers.

During the last ten days of the month there was held, by invitation of Mr. Moody, a conference of missionaries, superintendents, and officers of the American Sunday-school Union laboring in the Northwest. Discussions of every phase of the work occupied the conference during each afternoon, while the mornings were given by the missionaries to attending the lectures at the Bible Institute, and the evenings to the evangelistic services held under Mr. Moody's direction. The purpose of the conference was fourfold : first, to secure the advantages of two weeks' Bible study at the Institute; second, to learn from the methods of other workers how to reach people with the gospel invitation; third, to consider every phase of the work of the American Sunday-school Union as the missionaries were doing it, and to consider new plans for advance movements, and then to become acquainted with one another; fourth, to give the missionaries a rest by changing entirely their form of labor from the country to the city, and from the private study to the public lectures at the Institute. The coming of that army of about one hundred zealous, devoted workers proved a blessing to them and to the evangelistic movement, with which they came into close relations of sympathy and helpfulness during their ten days' stay in Chicago.

CHAPTER XXI.

A SPECIAL SOLDIERS' MEETING.

General Howard's Story.

ONE of the interesting and impressive special services in connection with the evangelistic movement was for the veteran survivors of our Civil War and their families. Cards of invitation were issued to all soldiers, Union and Confederate, who would accept them. This embraced Grand Army posts, and soldiers visiting the World's Fair from all parts of the land. The meeting was held in Central Music Hall on Sunday afternoon. A pressing call had been sent to the old, one-armed veteran warrior, Major-General O. O. Howard, to come and address this meeting, and aid in other services of the campaign. It was just like that noble Christian soldier to respond, as he did, with generous kindness and soldierly promptitude, to the call of his old army friend, Mr. Moody, and his former staff-officer, Major D. W. Whittle.

At the appointed hour a large congregation of veterans, with mothers, fathers, wives, children, widows, orphans, and friends of soldiers assembled in the great hall. On the platform with General Howard sat Major Whittle, the eminent evangelist, who had been on the general's staff during the Atlanta campaign and the march through Georgia, also Major Cole, another evangelist, Colonel Sexton, and others, including a representative of the British

112

Army, Lord Bennett, of London. Major Whittle presided
with characteristic tact and grace.

When the gray-haired major-general appeared on the
platform, with the significant empty sleeve dangling at
his side, the whole audience rose and greeted him with a
storm of hand-clapping. Professor George C. Stebbins
conducted the song service, and was assisted by Lord
Bennett, the Princeton Quartet, and a chorus choir. In
addition to solos and quartet songs, the hymn "America"
was sung by the congregation with deep feeling and thrilling effect. The dear old hymn, ringing out from the lips
of men and women who had given all they held most dear
for their country, took on new meaning as they sang it.
At General Howard's request, the congregation sang also
that stirring song, "Hold the fort," before he began to
speak.

As the general rose to speak, visibly affected, looking
every inch the true soldier of his country and of his Lord,
we remembered that he stood before us as the representative of a great army of heroes rapidly passing away, and
soon all to be gone. The thought seemed to touch every
.heart, and there were tears in many eyes and sobs in
many throats before a word was spoken. We knew the
old hero's history. He is the only surviving officer of the
five illustrious generals who commanded the Army of the
Tennessee—Grant, Sherman, McPherson, Howard, and
Logan. He was appointed to command after the death
of McPherson at Atlanta. He participated probably in
more of the prominent battles of the war than any officer
now living. He fought with McClellan in the Peninsular
campaign, losing his arm at Fair Oaks. He was on the
bloody fields of Fredericksburg, Chancellorsville, Antie-
tam, Gettysburg, and Chattanooga; went through the Atlanta campaign with its numerous battles; led the Army

of the Tennessee through Georgia and the Carolinas; and was an active participant in the last battle under Sherman in Fayetteville, N. C. He was honored with the thanks of the country through resolutions passed by Congress for his services on the field of Gettysburg.

The pronounced Christian character of General Howard was well known during the war, and has been so steadfastly maintained that he holds the confidence and love of the Christian people of the country, both North and South. General Sherman regarded him as the Stonewall Jackson of the Northern army, and gave him his confidence and affection to a very marked degree. Mr. Moody became acquainted with General Howard while in the Christian commission work connected with the soldiers, and their friendship and fellowship in Christian work has continued unbroken from the days of the war until now. They were companions in the memorable experiences on the steamship *Spree* last year, and were drawn yet closer together by the common danger shared and the mutual help afforded in the imminent peril through which they passed.

Major-General Howard commenced his address by saying that he had intended to speak of the loving-kindness of the Lord, but at the suggestion of his friend, Major Whittle, he would relate something about his experience in entering on the Christian life. "Perhaps," said he, in his modest way, "my simple story may help and cheer some one in the Christian way. My thoughts go back to the days of my youth. Oh, how much I have to be thankful for! We had bright, happy Sundays at my home, pure, good, uplifting days. When I left home to go to school my good mother always followed me with letters of motherly love and counsel and quotations from the Scriptures. Her favorite word for me was, 'Seek first the kingdom of God and his righteousness, and all these things shall be added unto you.' I knew not what it meant. But the words followed me and troubled me.

"You know there is a time in a man's life when he is affected with the measles of unbelief. It was so with me also. I spoke, as did others, slightingly of the Bible and of religion. One day a dear friend said to me, with mild and loving rebuke, 'Otis, if I were you, I wouldn't speak against the Bible, but just be a Christian.' These words, spoken in season, have been in my heart for forty-seven years. They brought me under conviction of sin.

"I had naturally a very ugly temper, quick and fierce. Major Whittle will hardly understand that. He has probably not found it out. I have tried to conquer it, by the grace of God, and get self-control. Mother continued to write to me, and I always wanted to please my mother. And I tried hard. It is only a short time ago that she passed away to her rest, not far from here. I am glad she lived to see her son a follower of Christ, according to her desire."

The general went on to tell of his life at West Point, and how he braved the ridicule of the cadets by going to religious services and doing work in the Sunday-school. He said it cost him more to take his stand and run the gauntlet of their scoffs and sneers than it did later to face the cannon and musketry of the battle-field. "But," said he, "I gripped my Bible, shut my teeth, and went, for mother's sake."

After the general had a family he read every morning a portion of Scripture before them, but did not pray publicly, until a time came when duty called him away from home. That day he read the Scriptures, and then fell on his knees and committed his loved ones to the keeping of God. But all this time he did not profess or claim to be a Christian. But one day he sat in a little church, on a back seat, in uniform. A little colored boy sat beside him, who fell asleep, and rested his head on the general's breast. He was proud and sensitive, and did not like the situation, but he always had a tender heart for children. The preacher soon came up to him, as to others in the congregation, with a personal appeal. "Which side would you rather be on—the Lord's side, or the side of those who mock Christ?" the preacher said. Promptly and resolutely the general's heart answered, "The Lord's side," and he rose, buttoned up his military coat, and marched down the aisle to the altar, where he knelt and committed himself to Christ. No change was experienced and no light received at the time of his committal, and he was in much perplexity as to how he might know of his acceptance by God and the pardon of his sins. This came to him the same night, while alone in his quarters.

A friend had sent him a copy of "The Life of Hedley Vicars." He read it with deep interest. He could not understand what was meant by the saying, so often repeated, "The blood of Jesus Christ his Son cleanseth us from all sin." He knelt down and asked God to show him what it meant, and God did it. "My soul was so happy," continued the general, "when God revealed to me the way of salvation by the blood of Jesus Christ, that I rejoiced with an unspeakable joy. That hour the gift of eternal life was consciously mine. Oh, the preciousness of that gift! There's no counting the value of it, and there's no discounting it!

"After this experience I wanted to be a chaplain, to seek the souls of men. But the war came. I responded to the call of my country, and went as conscientiously to the field of battle as to a prayer-meeting. On the eve of my first battle I became pale and weak at the sound of cannon and musketry and the roar of conflict. God was there, and I cried to him to give me strength to do my duty, and, quick as a flash, my courage and strength came, and I never faltered again in the face of any peril. I went forward with the confidence that I was doing God's will, and he never forsook me.

"When my dear friend, Captain Griffith, was shot down on the field of Gettysburg, we bore him to a house in the town to die. I went to see him once more, and read at his bedside the sweet words of Jesus, 'Let not your heart be troubled. . . . In my Father's house are many mansions: if it were not so, I would have told you. I go to prepare a place for you. And if I go to prepare a place for you, I will come again, and receive you unto myself; that where I am, there ye may be also.' At these words Griffith lifted his great, black eyes, looking into mine, and said: 'General Howard, I am not afraid to die. I am ready to go.' I bent over him and tenderly kissed his white forehead, bade him a last, loving good-by, and left him to die. I shall see my comrade again!" With a touching appeal to his hearers to be true soldiers of Jesus Christ, the general closed his affecting address.

At the close of the address Major Whittle bore a fellow-soldier's loving testimony to his comrade and to their common Lord. "I was privileged," said he, "to be with General Howard on his staff six months. I knew. him well. All who know him as I do will feel that he has been very modest in speaking of himself to-day. I never saw General Howard when he showed any weakness. in character. But of all the scenes where I was privileged to be with him, those errands of mercy among the sick and the dying, in hospitals and camp, most deeply impressed me. I remember one affecting case where a dying Confederate soldier was brought to Christ by the general's kind ministry.

"I want to add my testimony to that of General Howard, that the religion of Jesus Christ is a blessed reality, the greatest reality of life. I thank God that many of our comrades can also unite in this testimony. I commend unto you, comrades and friends, the verse that brought comfort and life to General Howard, "The blood of Jesus Christ his Son cleanseth us from all sin." I don't know why, but it is a soldier's verse. I could tell you of one and another who found peace in that word. Oh, my hope is in that precious truth and fact of the death of Jesus Christ for me."

After several more songs and prayer, and the relation of the story of his own conversion by Lord Bennett, the meeting was closed by Major Whittle, and the soldiers pressed forward to clasp once more the hand of their beloved commander and friend.

General Howard rendered very efficient service in a number of meetings in the Standard Theater and other places, pleading effectively with unsaved men and leading them to Christ for salvation. He greatly enjoyed his visit and labors in Chicago.

CHAPTER XXII.

IN VARIOUS LANGUAGES.

WHEN Mr. Moody began his World's Fair gospel work in Chicago he had it in his heart to bring the gospel message also to the ears of other various nationalities represented there, as well as to the English-speaking multitudes. Himself could not do this. His own preaching, by word of mouth, is confined to one language only—his strong, simple, lucid, limpid, terse, graphic English. But his heart yearned after the tens of thousands of Germans, French, Poles, Bohemians, Swedes, and other nationalities, and he rested not until they also heard the gospel at the mouth of evangelists in their own language.

Dr. J. W. Pindor, the eminent Polish scholar and preacher, of Silesia, was secured to preach to the Poles and the Germans. He came in May. He found it difficult to gain access to the Poles, who are mostly Catholics, but among the Germans the way opened more readily.

Mr. Joseph Rabinowitz, the Russian Hebrew apostle, came and preached the word to his Jewish brethren. He had meetings in the Chicago Hebrew Mission, the Ewing Street Congregational Church, and in other places. The presence and preaching of this remarkable Jewish Christian awakened much interest.

Rev. A. Skoogsbergh, known as "the Swedish Spurgeon," preached in the Swedish language, with great acceptance and success, to large audiences, week after week.

119

His services were held in the Swedish Mission Church, the Bethania Norwegian Church, the Swedish Tabernacle, the Chicago Avenue Church, and other places. Thousands of Swedes listened to the gospel preached with eloquence and power by their countryman, night after night and week after week, with unabated interest.

Rev. Pasteur Theodore Monod, from Paris, an able and eloquent French preacher, held special services for his countrymen in Chicago, preaching to them in the French language. He also preached sermons and delivered Bible lectures in the English language in various churches and in the Bible Institute.

Among the 60,000 Bohemians of the city a great deal of evangelistic work was done by various zealous workers, some of them from the Bible Institute. One of these evangelists, a young Bohemian from Kansas, labored among his countrymen with great zeal and patient endurance, in the face of insult and abuse, and even bodily injury. He preached in the open air, going from place to place, sometimes giving five-minute talks in as many as fifteen different places in one evening, with great crowds following him. Sometimes they stoned him, beat him, tore his clothes, threatened to kill him, and once his enemies had him arrested. Then the saloon-keepers hired ruffians and boys to drown his voice by all sorts of noises. But the work went on nevertheless, and the testimony of the gospel was given to many.

Dr. Stoecker among the Germans.

Among the German people a very fruitful work of evangelism was done. It was begun by Rev. Niclaus Boldt, of St. Paul, who with his devoted sister labored several months with good results. Services were held for some time in Christ Church, then transferred to Holmes's Hall. The evangelist was assisted by Professor Jacobs, who led the service of song. Later came Rev. Dr. Stoecker, former court preacher of Germany, and Count Bernstorff, who united their efforts in behalf of their countrymen. The coming of Dr. Stoecker especially was an event of much interest and importance. It was at the urgent request of Mr. Moody that the busy preacher, statesman, and reformer broke away from his work and came to take part in the Chicago campaign. He recognized in the voice of the American evangelist a Macedonian call in which the will of God was expressed. He conferred not with flesh and blood. It was another striking illustration of how the Lord of the harvest, to whom belong all the workers in the great world field, has given to his servant authority in the service of his kingdom to "say to one, Come, and he cometh; and to another, Go, and he goeth."

When it was known that Dr. Stoecker was coming to Chicago at Mr. Moody's call some of the secular press, East and West, took occasion to assail not only him and misrepresent his motives in coming to America, but also to reflect upon Mr. Moody for inviting him, and they predicted that his cause would suffer injury in consequence of it. Some of Mr. Moody's friends also were alarmed at the prospect of a conflict when the redoubtable German warrior, agitator, and reformer should join his forces. But Mr. Moody never wavered in his conviction, nor yielded his faith in the man he had called. He knew his man. He stood up bravely for him and stood loyally by him against the hostile press and the misgivings of friends. On the platform of the Central Music Hall, before an assembly of 3000 people, he said: "I thank God for the coming of this dear man of God. He is a man after my own heart. I don't know of any man in Christendom that I would rather have stand in the pulpit of our churches than this dear brother."

This decided attitude of Mr. Moody and his warm, hearty, brotherly recognition and indorsement of his guest as a man of God had a most happy effect. Dr. Stoecker honored this confidence of his friend by giving public assurance that he had not come to Chicago as an agitator, but as a preacher, to proclaim the gospel to his brethren. His first public address, which was eagerly awaited by both friends and foes, soon set at rest the fears of the former, and silenced the voices of the latter, while it vindicated the wisdom and sound judgment of Mr. Moody.

During three weeks Dr. Stoecker went in and out among us, as a man of God without guile and without reproach, preaching the gospel in beautiful simplicity, sweetness, and power in various churches, halls, and tents, and addressing immense audiences in the Central Music Hall, on four memorable occasions, with surpassing eloquence. Indifference, prejudice, and opposition alike bowed beneath the conquering spell of his magnetic personality, his clear, keen, luminous, wide-reaching thought, and his captivating, triumphant oratory. Some of his hearers will not soon forget how he brought them face to face with the highest and noblest ideals of life and character, and with the overawing realities and solemnities of eternity; how he appealed to the German heart by all that is best and most inspiring in the old national life, character, and history; how he touched with masterly skill and power the mystic chords of memory that bind every true German heart to the old home-land beyond the sea; and how faithfully, as with the ken and courage of a prophet, and the wisdom of one taught of God through the lessons of history, he set forth the evils and dangers that beset the path of this great republic in its career of development, and pointed out the only security for personal, individual, social, and national life in the religion of the Lord Jesus Christ. Some will long remember how persuasively he appealed to the sons of the old fatherland to show themselves worthy of the new fatherland to which they had come, by seeking the highest good of the places where they dwelt, and to aspire to the better Fatherland in that unseen world toward which all men haste.

Some of the most deeply impressive meetings addressed by Dr. Stoecker were an immense gathering in one of the tents, on a week-day afternoon, and two remarkable mothers' meetings in Holmes's Hall, when from 500 to 600 German mothers listened with overwhelming emotion to the burning words of the speaker. Of these meetings Dr. Stoecker has spoken in terms of praise and thanksgiving to God.

The last address of Dr. Stoecker, before an audience of 3000 in the Central Music Hall, was his crowning triumph on the Chicago platform. His soul was all aglow with the contagious emotion of high and holy thought, which diffused itself through the immense multitudes like an electric atmosphere, in which the speaker's words had free course to run and be glorified.

Such a discourse was never before heard in Chicago. It was unreportable. There was in it an undertone of irresistible pathos, and breathing through it the irrepressible yearning of the speaker's heart for the salvation and highest welfare of his brethren, and the peace and prosperity of the city and the land wherein they had found a home. It was as though the spirit of the old fatherland itself had found an embodiment and a voice to speak to its emigrant children on the shores of this New World.

It is interesting to notice what estimate the German

secular press has formed of Dr. Stoecker in his noble championship of Christianity in Chicago. A fair specimen expression will be found in an editorial of one of the ablest and most influential German dailies of the West, which has no sympathy with the religion of Jesus Christ. The article is remarkable for its recognition of the high character and abilities of the illustrious preacher, and of the work he performed in Chicago. Among other most appreciative and laudatory things it says: "For Dr. Stoecker's three weeks' work in Chicago he certainly deserves the warm appreciation of the German-Americans."

In taking leave of Mr. Moody and his co-workers, Dr. Stoecker was deeply moved, and responded with full heart to the brotherly kindness of which he had become the recipient.

He went away with a strong desire and earnest hope to return again within two years, if God permit, to help his brethren in their upward striving after the best and highest things for the life that now is and for that which is to come.

Mr. Moody himself visited the meetings of the various nationalities, although unable to understand their languages, and also preached once for the Swedes, for the Bohemians, and for the Germans, many of whom could understand and enjoy his racy English, and all of whom could understand the spirit with which he spoke.

The impression made by the meetings throughout the city on other nationalities from non-Christian lands was by no means limited to the languages in which the word was preached and sung. As an indication of the general interest in the English services, the following note, addressed to Mr. Moody, will serve as a sample of many which were daily received at his office. The note runs thus:

"DEAR MR. MOODY: Please send me twelve tickets to your meeting in the Haymarket Theater, on next Sunday morning, for a company of Japanese gentlemen, representing their country at the Columbian Exposition. They say they greatly desire to attend the services. They would be pleased to have seats together."

CHAPTER XXIII.

GLIMPSES OF TENT WORK.

In this rapid survey of the six months' work in Chicago a very prominent place should be given to what might be called the tent brigade. Reference has already been made to the tent work, whose value can hardly be over-estimated. It has furnished an answer to the oft-repeated question, "How shall we reach the masses with the gospel?"

The uninformed reader, who has never attended one of those meetings, will appreciate a little outline sketch of a typical tent meeting, such as have been held for seven summers in various parts of Chicago, under the Chicago Evangelization Society, of which the Bible Institute is a part. During the World's Fair season five of these tents were in constant use, accomplishing an incalculable amount of good.

A Specimen Evening Service.

A participant thus describes an evening service in one of the tents:

After supper in the men's department of the Bible Institute about one hundred men are on their knees for a few moments. Brief, burning, pointed prayers ascend. God is counted on to stand by them in their work. Then, rising, they scatter to mission and tent, going in some

cases four, five, and even six miles, each with his Bible
and little package of tracts, those containing plenty
of Scripture being preferred. Meanwhile, in the ladies'
home, fifty young women have been making similar prep-
arations. One party is going to the big tent on Milwaukee Avenue, where Mr. Schiverea is holding meetings.
On the street-car no time is lost. A young woman opposite speaks to the tired shop-girl at her side, opens her
Bible, and points her to Him who said, "Come unto me,
all ye that labor and are heavy laden, and I will give you
rest;" but the girl must get off at the next block. She
slips the tract "God's Word to You" into her hand with
a kind pressure, and asks her to read it. A pleasant smile
and a good-night, and the seed is sown. Meanwhile the
young men are not idle. A tract is handed to a fellow-
passenger, a kind word is spoken, and soon they, too,
are talking of that wonderful Saviour. A man on the
platform has secured the attention of the conductor, who
seems under conviction. But we have reached our destination, and step from the cars.

Before us is the tent, brilliantly lighted. We enter, and
overhead is a great arch of canvas, supported by three
center-poles and smaller ones about the sides—an auditorium accommodating 1300 people, and seated with canvas benches.

The little party kneel in prayer for the presence and
power of the Holy Spirit. Then some take their places
upon the platform to sing the gospel, some stand ready
to welcome and seat the audience, and others go out upon
the street, with cards of invitation to bring in passers-by.

From our seat on the platform we watch the audience
come in. First, a hesitating group of ragged little ones,
then some young "toughs," with mischief in their faces,
are passed from one usher to another, who will keep his

eye upon them. Next a mother with a baby in her arms, a laboring-man in gingham shirt and no collar, fathers and mothers with their little ones—so they gather—largely an audience of respectable working-people, for this is the character of the neighborhood; but the "tough" element is not wanting also. The blue, coat of a policeman seen at the door makes it easy to preserve order. The police of Chicago have proved good friends of this work, and some of their hearts have been found tender as well as brave.

A gospel hymn opens the meeting, and how these people sing! A solo from an Institute lady, full of the gospel message, more hymns, a duet, prayer, and the evangelist begins to speak. Tenderly, lovingly, he deals with the people; unsparingly he deals with their sins. The trace of the actor still lingers in his graphic illustrations, largely drawn from his own experience; but so anxious is he that all be to the glory of God that he uses these with more and more care every year.

The address is short, and a hymn of invitation to Christ is sung by the same soloist as before, and then the speaker begins to ask those who wish to turn from a life of sin to God to rise. Here and there they rise to their feet, the Institute workers marking them carefully. Then the leader says that all may go who wish to do so, but that a short after-meeting will be held for those who choose to remain. A large part of the audience stay, and the workers thread their way among them, sitting down by those who have risen, and trying from the Word of God to show the way of salvation, often finding among those who linger deep conviction of sin, without the courage to rise and manifest the interest felt. At a late hour the party are once more on the cars, singing the Lord's songs as they take the long ride home.

A Specimen All-day Meeting.

A World's Fair visitor who witnessed the extraordinary spectacle of one of the enthusiastic all-day meetings in Evangelist Schiverea's big tent gives this vivid picture of the scene:

All day, from nine o'clock in the morning till eleven at night, the tent was crowded with working-people singing gospel hymns and hearing vigorous, common-sense talking by the leading evangelists of the day.

It was a singular spectacle. The vaulted ceiling of the church was replaced by the swaying folds of tent-cloth; the clustered pillars were exchanged for leaning tent-poles; there were canvas-bottomed benches in place of cushioned pews; a cabinet organ was substituted for the stately instrument of the church; instead of a velvet carpet there were shavings strewed on the ground, and in place of colored windows the sides of the tent were all open, so that the daylight streamed in and the songs of choir and people echoed out on the busy streets.

It was no dress occasion for the audience. They came in their every-day clothes—hard-working men, out-of-work men, old men and young boys, strangers in the city, neighbors of the tent, women with crowing babes in their arms and little children clinging about them, and young girls in gay bonnets; while here and there were the students of Mr. Moody's Bible Institute. The day was warm, but the audience was patient and attentive, though the tent was so crowded that many were obliged to stand outside. Some even mounted lumber piles and looked over the heads of the audience.

Fifteen hundred people attended the morning services. At nine o'clock Mr. Schiverea conducted a praise service with song, testimony, and prayer, closing with numerous requests for prayers. At ten o'clock the Torrey Quartet sang, and after a solo by D. B. Towner, R. A. Torrey gave a practical talk on Christian service and growth. After an intermission the next hour was begun by a hymn by the Oberlin Quartet, then Mr. Moody took the platform, and began his address by saying that he was going to talk about a promise. He spoke in substance as follows:

"Christ left so many promises and such good ones you can't tell which is the best. Some people don't believe them, some think they are too good to be true. Some think they were never meant to be believed, and some think God can't fulfil them. Most of the promises are on conditions, but the promise of Jesus was not on conditions. Nothing on earth or in hell could have prevented his coming. Some promises were to the Jews, and not to us; but this promise is to all alike. If we don't appropriate it, it isn't worth anything to us. The promise is this: 'Come unto me, all ye that labor and are heavy laden, and I will give you rest.' The want of the human heart is rest: theaters, saloons, and pleasures mean the search for rest in pleasure.

"Men are doomed to disappointment if they try to drown sorrow in pleasure. If I wanted to find men who had rest I would not go among millionaires, or fashion-slaves, or politicians. When God made your heart and mine, he made it too big for this world. The world can't fill it. We need two worlds. I'll tell you where to find those who've got rest. Go among the disciples of Jesus. Come to Jesus, and you will get rest. That's my experience. You will find it at the cross. Come, and you'll get it.

"I'm not going to tell you what 'come' means. I used to work hard to make people see what it was to come; but I don't do that any more; I've gone out of the business. The first thing a baby learns is to come—nothing mysterious about it! The Bible is full of it. As you follow it through, the voice grows louder and louder. Thank God for the call! Come with your sins. Your sins may keep you out of heaven, but they can't keep you from Christ. Why don't you come, chains and all? Jesus can set you free from your sins. Jesus can destroy even the appetite for drink. He means not you goody people, but you sinners.

"Now, to Christians. Christ is not only a sin-bearer, he's a burden-bearer. Let the Christians come too, and get rest. People don't do that. People embalm their sorrows. Cast your sorrows on him. People drop their sorrows while they listen to a preacher or a singer, and then they pick them right up again. Cast your care on him. He says, 'I'll give you rest.' May God write this on the heart of every one here!"

An hour's intermission gave time for dinner, and neighborly friends entertained those who had come from a distance. At one o'clock a consecration meeting was held, and then the assembly was addressed by "Abe" Mulkey, the Texas evangelist.

During the next hour a children's meeting was held by Major Whittle. Mr. Jacobs's solo was followed by a sweet duet by two little golden-haired girls. Then Mr. Jacobs stood a little six-year-old baby on a chair and she sang a solo, to the delight of the audience. After a trio by girls and considerable congregational singing, Major Whittle gave an illustrated talk. What the major said was so forcible and clear that it reached the older people quite as effectually as it did the children.

After a quartet by the Torrey singers the Scotch evangelist, Rev. John McNeill, made an address. He began with some pleasantry at the expense of his own nationality, and then announced as his theme the story of the man with the withered hand, taken from the third chapter of Mark. In substance he said :

"The Saviour's interest centered in the man with the withered hand—in him of all the crowd of the synagogue. The Lord loves a fellow that's down. Jesus said, 'Stand forth.' Then he said, 'Stretch forth thy hand.' Two words did the business. The man stood forth. Play the man if you're going to be a Christian. You're brazen-faced enough as a sinner. You don't care who sees you going into the saloon, but you're ashamed to be seen coming to Jesus.

"You go to the devil without a blush; don't be ashamed to be a Christian. May God give you courage. When the man stood forth Jesus made short work of the withered hand. They may scoff you into hell. They can't scoff you out. Mind you, if I'm saying sharp things, my heart's warm. God's gospel works not to cut to pieces, but to cut out the evil. Stand forth in the midst. Don't try to sneak into heaven. Resist the devil and he'll flee from you. He's a bigger coward than you are, and that's saying a good deal. One man with Jesus is a splendid majority. The man with the withered hand might have thought Jesus an impostor. Look to Jesus—don't look at your sins. Taking Jesus at his word saves me for-evermore.

"Now, I want to follow the man home. There is an old tradition that the man with the withered hand was a stone-mason spoiled for stone-cutting.

"Imagine the scene when the man went home to his family with his withered hand restored! The explana-tion was all in one word—Jesus. My God, what a family blessing salvation is! And God let the man live on to prove his restoration. God doesn't whisk a man away to heaven as soon as he's converted. He keeps him alive to let him work. Then that man works to the glory of God.

"The sermon's preached. Now it's to do it. We can't be born full-grown, but we may be born now. Now, away home and confess Jesus."

Another splendid audience spent the evening with Mr. Schiverea. The evangelist spoke on Peter's attempt to walk on the water, his faithlessness, failure, and rescue. The text was, " Lord, save me! "—the earnest cry of an anxious soul. The preacher emphasized the fact that Peter cried in time of danger. Many a man is led within the Saviour's reach by force of circumstances. Again, Peter cried when he was just beginning to sink, instead of waiting, as most men do, till he had sunk altogether. It was a cry of utter helplessness. The sooner a man realizes his own helplessness the sooner will he lay hold of God's almighty help. Moreover, Peter's cry was earnest, and not only earnest, but personal: "Lord, save me!" Best of all, it was a cry that brought instantaneous deliverance.

Considerably after ten o'clock the lights were put out. Neighboring saloon-keepers, it is said, say that the Moody mission is ruining their business.

CHAPTER XXIV.

INCIDENTS OF TENT WORK.

THE work in the tents is rich in incidents of the most encouraging character, and many an unwritten romance of providence and grace has there come to the knowledge of the workers. For the sake of brevity we will give only a few of the ordinary incidents which have come to our knowledge. Mr. Schiverea says: "I met a man one night who seemed to be very much troubled, and I soon discovered that he was a drinking man. He had spent from fifty cents to a dollar and a half for drink every day for ten years, and at that time had in his pocket a bottle of medicine to cure the appetite. After talking with him awhile he saw that Christ was what he wanted. He knelt down and confessed his sins, praying that God would forgive him for breaking his poor old mother's heart, and for grieving his wife, who is now dead, and for neglecting to support his daughter, and promising, if God would forgive him, to be a better man by his help. The next day while at work his foreman asked him what was the matter with him. He said that he was at the tent the night before and had taken Jesus as his Saviour. I met him about a week afterward and he told me it was the happiest week of his whole life, and that he had spent no more money for liquor. The foreman had told him, 'If God can save a miserable drunkard like you, he can save me,' and promised to come to the tent."

134

A horse-jockey who had been racing for ten years was converted. A rumseller's wife came in and listened to the speaking, but said, though she would like to be a Christian, she could not while her husband was in that business. A rumseller, sobered by the preaching of the gospel, admitted that he would like to be a Christian but could not, as he was selling rum near the tent, and felt that God could not save him while in that business, but that he would be out of the business in a short time, as he was tired of it, knew it was wrong, and could see the awful harm it was doing. He went away promising to decide for Christ.

Two young girls were found in the back of the tent one night, one of whom was crying. The evangelist spoke to her about her soul's salvation. She had nothing to say. A night or two later he again spoke to her, when she answered, "I am only a rumseller's daughter." "But Jesus loves rumsellers' daughters, and is ready to save them." She answered, "I can never forgive you; you called my father a thief." "Oh, no, I did not." "Yes, you said they stole the joy and peace out of the home, they stole character, they stole manhood, and they stole money from their customers." "Well, isn't that true?" She looked up into the face of the evangelist, and, bursting into tears, said, "Oh, yes, it is true!" "Is not your mother a Christian?" "No; and my father is a Roman Catholic." She was urged to take Christ as her Saviour and try to bring in father and mother, and in a groping fashion tried to do so. The next night an Institute lady was on her knees with those two girls, and so manifest was the power of God that it seemed as if the whole place about them were holy. Later the girl met the evangelist and said: "It is all right now. I am trusting Jesus, and my friend is too."

When the invitation was given one evening in Mr. Schiverea's tent, the first man on his feet was a Spaniard. Mr. Schiverea went to him and said, "Do you want Jesus Christ?" Said he, "If I had not wanted Jesus Christ I would not have risen, sir. You have got something that I do not know anything about, and I want it. I was in a saloon and my wife called me out and said, 'I have taken Jesus as my Saviour. I was down at the mothers' meeting at Moody's church and took Jesus to be my Saviour, and now I want you to come with me to the tent.' I came, sir, and I want what you people have got. Aren't you a Spaniard?" "I am of Spanish parentage, but do not speak the language." "Oh, I wish you did, I am so full in here," putting his hands on his breast. This man, who speaks several languages and is very intelligent, came to Christ like a little child. He had been reared in the Catholic Church, but like many others, had lost faith in it, and was practically an infidel.

In the great throng that filled Major Whittle's tent one evening was a wild, reckless, dissipated Western cowboy. He had hitched his pony to a fence near by, and spent the afternoon in drinking and carousal. Passing the tent in the evening, he turned in to see what was going on. After the sermon Major Whittle engaged him in conversation. In answer to a question the man said he liked what he had heard, and would like "to catch on" if he could. He was evidently a stranger to religious things. After faithful dealing with the poor sinner, the evangelist finally got him to consent to kneel down with him and pray. "I have never done anything like this," he said. The major encouraged him to pray as best he could, and the poor fellow cried out, "O God, I believe in you! I believe you are up there, and I am down here, a poor sinner, and I want to be saved." Another brand plucked out of the fire.

At one of the tent meetings the following, among other testimonies, were given. A former criminal and tramp said: "My father kept a saloon; I was brought up on the street, had no Christian training, and learned to do everything bad—smoke, drink, gamble, and steal. I learned the barber trade, got in bad company, and was in jail nine times. I was chased from Duluth by detectives. For a long time I was a feather-weight prize-fighter. When I came to Chicago I was a tramp in rags. I began to frequent city missions, and all by myself I made up my mind to become a Christian, though I was led to do so by the lives of Christian people."

A colored student told the following story: "I came from Africa a few years ago. I entered a dime museum to give exhibitions of African customs. After that I used to dance barefooted on broken glass and hot iron in a show. There I began a bad life. In a mission in Scranton, Pa., I was converted and left the dime museum forever."

A young man said: "My home is in New Zealand. I was converted there, and there I heard of the Bible Institute, and I have come to America to study under Mr. Moody."

CHAPTER XXV.

ONE OF THE TENT WORKERS.

MR. FERDINAND SCHIVEREA, who has for four summers been identified with tent work in Chicago, has peculiar qualifications which well entitle him to the commanding place he holds in that service. The following brief sketch of this successful soul-saver may fittingly follow the description of a work in which he has been the most prominent figure.

One night, as he was leaving an opera-house door, during his preparation for the stage, his pious mother met him with these words: "Son, I have good news for you: you are going to be converted and preach the gospel before I die." It was a startling, disquieting, extraordinary message to hear, with the applause of the pleasure-seeking audience still ringing in his ears, and the flash and glitter of the footlights still before him. The words sank deep into his heart. He made no reply, but silently took the loving mother on his arm and went homeward. The more he thought of it the more he was convinced that accumulation of sorrows and struggles, brought about by the dissipation of his father and his own wayward life, had shattered her mind, and now she had gone insane. But this conviction of her mental state soon passed away, and while he could not accept her prophecy as true, it nevertheless unsettled his own mind. He sought again and again to recover his former buoyancy of spirits, daubed on more burned cork, mimicked the more, but

138

to no successful end. The arrow of conviction had gone home to his heart.

At this time Mr. Moody was holding a series of gospel meetings in Brooklyn. He was providently led to one of these services, and then the Spirit of God took hold on him mightily. He had no rest for days, and finally passed out into the light a saved man. His first impulse was to "tell mother." Returning home at once, he found his mother, who had been reading the Word, sitting in her chair asleep. With a tender caress he awoke her, and with tears of joy told her God had saved him. Then the dear old saint put her arms about her new-born son and said: "I have asked God for this, dear child; I have given you to God, and he has just done what he said he would if I only would believe."

Ferdinand Schiverea now, like all truly converted souls, began to work for his master *at home.* His first effort was to lead his brothers to Christ. No sooner was he converted than he reached out for the neighbors. This he sought to accomplish by fitting up a small rear room in his poor home. The converted brother would go on the sidewalk and invite the people into the improvised chapel, where Ferdinand welcomed them. When they had thus secured an audience the meeting began. Every night for months the good work went on, and thus step by step he was led to a grander work.

During this period, and for several years thereafter, the young man labored hard at manual labor to support his young wife and mother. But while he was thus employed with his hands his mind and soul were being fed on the Word of God. His work for four years' time was in a large basement of a furniture house, where he packed goods for shipment. In this basement was a coal cellar, and here, in the unemployed time and at the noon hour, he locked himself in, and in this theological seminary—a very university of adversity—alone with God, on his knees, educated his soul and mind for future usefulness. Having left school at an early age, he did not even secure the advantage of a common school education.

The first work that God especially blessed him in was that in the city of Brooklyn, N. Y., where for twelve months he held meetings nearly every night. The place that was there marked the black spot was turned into one of the brightest places of the city. He has labored in some of the principal cities and towns of the United States, also most of the cities and towns of Canada.

Earnest, eager for souls, brave to declare the whole truth, unselfish and full of wisdom and the power of the Holy Ghost, he is winning many for the kingdom. Warmhearted, faithful, and loyal, he preaches a gospel for the masses in plain, simple terms, with homely illustrations and warm-hearted application.

He is eminently a man of prayer. Simple, clear, and direct in his appeal to the throne of grace, he at once wins the attention and sympathy of his hearers. Although he is a power with the common people while on the platform, it is in the after-meetings that the man's true character and spirit are manifest. Here he at once goes to the heart and life of the sin-sick soul. He often puts one of his great strong arms around some poor drunkard or fallen man, and with the other points him to the great Burden-bearer of a weary world. By the very force of his earnestness and loving pleading, many break down in an agony of tears and at once take the Christ held out. It is the one consuming passion of his life to bring sinners to the Christ who has saved him and kept him in all his ways, and God is honoring his faith and zeal with constant success.

CHAPTER XXVI.

WORK AMONG THE YOUNG PEOPLE.

No survey of the World's Fair evangelistic movement would be complete without taking account of the special work done for children and young people. It is true that in many or most of the great meetings held by the evangelists there were many children present who shared in the benefits thereof. But if it had not been for the special meetings held for the children, a large measure of the most blessed results of the great campaign would have been lost.

During the season of tent work there were always large numbers of young people present in the meetings. It was one of the most pleasing sights to see entire families, from the oldest to the youngest, parents and children, thronging to those meetings, day after day, month after month. And in many cases they were brought by families into the ark of salvation, oftentimes the little ones leading the way.

Major D. W. Whittle, Ferd. Schiverea, and others of the tent workers made a specialty of work for the children, using the stereopticon and illustrative teaching. Major Whittle, who has years of fruitful experience of such work, devoted much of his time to this department of service, and realized constant results in happy conversions. All other workers among the children were rewarded with fruits of their labors. Not by any means the least of the good results accomplished by showing a special interest in the children has been the influence and effect upon the parents. In many cases this has proved to be the most direct, and perhaps in some instances the only way, to reach the hearts of the parents and older members of the families.

In the month of June Mr. George D. Mackay, of New York, devoted ten consecutive nights to the children in the Chicago Avenue Church. It was the preaching of the gospel in the most direct and simple way, in effect, holding up steadily before the eyes and hearts of the assembly the face of the Lord Jesus Christ. The method was to throw upon a canvas by a stereopticon a series of beautiful pictures illustrating the life of Christ, copied from the best paintings of old and modern masters. As these scenes passed before the eyes of the children Mr. Mackay read, with but little comment or explanation, from a harmonized arrangement of the gospels those portions bearing upon the scenes presented. The pictures and the story did their quiet work on the young minds and hearts, and a number were brought to Jesus. So great was the interest in the meetings that crowds stood awaiting the opening of the doors each night, and the building was soon packed to overflowing.

On the 1st of August Miss B. B. Tyson, of Washington, D. C., commenced her work among the young people in connection with the campaign. She came with the reputation of a successful leader and worker. From the 1st of August to the close of the campaign, October 31st, she held daily meetings in churches, chapels, halls, or tents, with an aggregate attendance of 28,550, at a low estimate. And for another month following the close of the campaign she continued her daily meetings with even larger attendance and greater results. About 11,500 people at-

tended the meetings of the month, and many were converted, not only children, but young men and women, as
well as fathers and mothers.

In Miss Tyson's meetings the children soon learned to
coöperate heartily with her, and they proved to be good
workers in bringing others to the services. At one place
there were 300 strangers brought in by them in the course
of one week. The evening congregations were usually
composed more than half of grown people. The fathers
and mothers were often brought in by the children who
had come and found Christ, and in many cases these
parents also were brought to the feet of the Saviour.

Miss Tyson deals in the most direct, simple, straight-
forward manner with her hearers. She has well learned
the high art of attracting, interesting, controlling, and
influencing congregations of young people without reac-
tionary tricks and devices. She preaches the plain, simple
gospel of Christ, in the power of the Holy Spirit, with
chalk pictures and words that go straight to mind and
heart. The object always is the salvation of the hearer.
"At the close of her addresses," says Miss Anna Pierson,
one of her assistants, "there follows a second or after
meeting for personal dealing with individual souls. There
is no fixed plan for this meeting, but it is varied according to circumstances, as the Lord directs. At one time it
is given up to testimony or prayer, when all Christians,
both young and old, take part. At another time opportunity is given to the unconverted to take a stand for
Christ, either by the raising of the hand or by coming
forward. After this the workers talk and pray with each
one separately. After the close of a mission in a place
some worker is appointed to look after the converts, and
in some places meetings are held for them once a week, to
give them spiritual help in their Christian life."

Incidents.

The following incidents, related by Miss Pierson, will serve as indications of what is constantly occurring in connection with Miss Tyson's work:

"At one of the meetings a man seventy-five years of age was converted. He said that the last time he had prayed was when he was a child at his mother's knee.

"One night a father arose to thank the Lord that his four boys had all been brought to the Saviour during the meetings.

"During the after-meeting one evening, the leader noticed two boys sitting together talking earnestly. On inquiring whether they were Christians, one of them replied that he had been saved at the meeting two nights before. His companion, he said, wanted to be a Christian too, but no one had come to tell him how. As no one had come, this two-day-old Christian boy had told his companion just how he had accepted Christ. Then they had prayed together, and the second boy believed that he too had received a new heart. On questioning the new convert the leader found that he seemed to understand clearly what he had done, and to be truly trusting in Jesus Christ.

"An unconverted mother was brought in one night by one of the children. She was a moral woman, and had never felt herself a sinner. She was convicted and converted, and went home and told her unconverted husband. He came with her the following night, and he too decided for Christ. The next day, while at work and talking with some companions, he began to emphasize one of his statements with an oath. He stopped suddenly, for he said he felt that he could not take the name of his Saviour in vain. Then for the first time he felt that he was indeed a changed man. The next day, for the first time, he gave

God thanks at the table for the food provided, and set up a family altar.

"At a testimony meeting a mother arose and gave thanks for the great change in her children and home since the meetings began. At the same meeting a little girl gave a very beautiful testimony in the following words: 'I used to think I was very happy when I had a new book given me, or a new gift of any kind, but I never was so happy in my life as I was the day Jesus gave me a new heart.'"

"It is pleasing to see," says Miss Tyson, in speaking of her work during the oppressive heat of summer, "and it causes in us rejoicing and thanksgiving to God that so many dear children are drawn to our religious meetings these afternoons when the heat is so oppressive, and the parks afford so much greater physical comfort, and the streets are alive with attractions. What a privilege to work for Jesus and to feed his lambs! In many cases fathers and mothers come with their children. Is this not a case in which 'a little child shall lead them'? These parents would not thus place themselves under the influence of the word but for the abounding interest of their little ones in these meetings. At one meeting there were eight baby-coaches in the tent, babies sleeping quietly while their mothers enjoyed the service.

"One of our tents is now located where it was two years ago, at which time quite a number of young people professed faith in Christ, and the genuineness and permanence of that work are indicated in the fact that at our very first meeting a father gave thanks to God for the conversion of his two sons two years ago, and twenty-four young people, from ten to seventeen years of age, have testified that they also decided for the Saviour at the meetings held two years ago."

Careful observers have been thankful to see that the work among the children never fails to yield large returns, perhaps exceeding any other form of religious work. It has been remarked that as the tents go back, year after year, into the same neighborhoods, children who were converted in years previous are found living lives which shame those of many older Christians, testifying for Christ, enduring much self-denial, and often persecution.

One of the Meetings.

One of the leaders gives us this spirited picture of one of the children's meetings, the closing one of a series in the tents:

"Sitting on the front seat is a dear, white-faced, flaxen-haired Swede, eyes as blue as the sky, dressed as she would have been for a protrait, hair braided all over her head, clean as a pink, quiet as a mouse, with hands folded in her lap, all ready to listen.

"Next her is a dusky Italian; she has no stockings, no shoes, dress all torn, face all aglow, with eyes full of pathos, face full of eager attention, love for Jesus shining through all, never still a moment, but as sweet as the fairer girl next her.

"Next her is a nice little Scotch girl, with a baby sister cuddled close to her side. She is as modest as a violet, and has just come over. I asked her how many brothers and sisters she had, and when she said eleven, I exclaimed, 'Oh, my! how did mamma bring you all over—wasn't she afraid some of you would get lost?' Looking into my face with eyes clear and truthful, she answered, 'Oh, yes! mamma was afraid, so she tied us all together on shipboard.' She loves Jesus now, and will take better care of brother.

"Next behind come flashing Irish eyes—a boy and girl of eleven and twelve—ready either for smiling or weeping, yet underneath all determined to be Christians. Then come a couple of children from the sunny South, with skins darker than Italians, but with faces grown serious as they listen to the gospel.

"The boys answer a similar description, and some of them are to be the future aldermen of Chicago. If they are truly converted the city will be blessed.

"The last day comes. For four weeks hearts have been touched and souls have been born again, and now comes the parting. The tent moves to another place. The faces are all serious, tender, and brave. We sing the well-learned songs. We pray, asking God to be their Shepherd. Poor little lambs! The wolves are after them all too soon!

"Then our evangelist, Mr. Williams, talks. The quiet is oppressive as he advises them to read and pray and live close to Jesus. The girls' choir recites 'I will lift up mine eyes unto the hills.' We sing 'God be with you till we meet again,' and the August tent work for children is ended."

Impressive Experiences.

One of the lady workers of the Bible Institute gives this bright bit out of her happy experiences among the children:

"A pull at my dress, and I turn to find a little eight-year-old girl standing by me in the tent. Her little face is all eagerness as she looks into mine, and she holds tightly by the hand a tiny girl, whom she tells me is Josie, and she is 'most six.'

"Hurriedly but sweetly she tells me that her heart has been clean since yesterday, and she wants her little sister to have hers cleansed too; that it was such a black heart before because in it was no love for the dear Jesus whose blood could make it clean; that it is, oh, so nice to have it clean, and that Josie must have hers washed too.

"In her eagerness she keeps pushing the little sister in front of her, but answering all my questions herself.

"'Oh, yes, miss, she knows her heart hasn't been made clean.' 'She knows Jesus' blood will make it clean.' 'She won't let any black spots get on it, 'cause Jesus will help her—we will ask him together. I won't let her forget to ask. I will tell her about it all the time.' 'Oh, please, she isn't too little, is she, if I keep telling her all the time she mustn't let any black spots get on her heart?'

"Drawing the little one close to me, I tell her of that first missionary, who, after that experience of a few hours spent with Jesus in a little hut in the wilderness of Judea, 'first findeth his own brother' and brought him to Jesus.

"With a happy and contented smile she listens, and then says to me, 'Then I am a little missionary, too. Isn't it nice to bring folks to Jesus? I am going to bring some more.'

"And as she goes out of the tent—so happy in her mission—an earnest prayer goes up from my heart for her, that it may always be natural for her to tell of this which so fills her heart as for a flower to unfold, or a fountain to bubble forth, and that, thus telling, she may find and bring many to him."

Little Clara.

Miss Poxon has a rich store of precious experiences in her blessed and fruitful work with the children. In the following striking sketch she gives us a glimpse of "the way it works." She says:

"One afternoon in the children's meeting, after all the

workers had gone, Mr. S. noticed two little girls sitting on the front seat. I went to them, and kneeling down in front of them, I said, 'And what do these girlies want? Do they want to be Christians?' The larger one, whose name was Clara, said, 'Oh, yes, we have wanted to be Christians this long time, but nobody asked us.' Taking them to God's Word, I showed them how much he wanted them, even so much as to give his Son for them. Then we knelt in prayer, Clara' praying herself, asking God to give her a clean heart.

"We arose, and then I explained 'believe,' 'receive,' 'confess,' telling her to be sure and tell mamma when she returned home. I held in my hand a Testament. She asked me for one, saying, 'Will you mark the lesson we had to-day?' The lesson was, 'Lord, save me,' 'Lord, help me,' 'Lord, remember me.' I marked each place, and several others, for her. She promised to read it every day. She returned the next day. We had a testimony meeting, and she was the first on her feet, saying, 'I gave my heart to Jesus yesterday, and he helps me.' She came every day that week, to be an inspiration to the leader of the children's meeting.

"The next Tuesday I missed that bright face. Wednesday it rained. Thursday she was not there. Friday was the last day of the children's meetings in that place. I looked for the darling, but had not time to go to her home before meeting. As soon as it closed I sent three girls with two picture-cards for the two sisters. Coming back in a few moments, they said, 'Why, Clara is dead! They have just come from her funeral.' I went over to the house; found it all true. She was taken ill on Monday, and asked for 'teacher' several times. Her mother did not know my address, and Wednesday it rained so badly she thought we would not be there. Thursday she called her mother to her, asking her to sing 'I think when I read that sweet story of old,' and said, 'Mamma, that verse about his hands on my head, sing that.' The mother did not know it. Then she asked for her Testament, and said, 'Read, mamma, "Lord, save me," "Lord, help me," "Lord, remember me." I saw that little Testament, all covered with her finger-marks, where she had read. She became unconscious soon after, and died that evening, saying, as she passed away, 'Suffer the little children to come unto me, and forbid them not, for of such is the kingdom of heaven.' How thankful I am for that one more precious soul in heaven."

Another Zaccheus.

Another incident related by Miss Poxon is so suggestive and encouraging that we may not pass it by without sharing it with our readers. She says:

"One afternoon in the tent we had had a lesson about three steps to a saved world: the first was 'Listen,' the second, 'Receive,' and the third, 'Follow.' We talked about 'Listen,' came to 'Receive,' and forgot entirely what to say. The lesson prepared had entirely slipped out of mind. Pausing a moment and asking the Lord to give us the lesson, a picture of mothers' meeting came before our eyes, and we heard Mrs. Capron's voice saying, 'He received him joyfully.' So, telling the story of Zaccheus and the tree instead of the one forgotten, we went on with the lesson, closing with an after-meeting. In the after-meeting one of the students called me, saying, as he introduced a boy, 'This is Zaccheus. He has given his heart to Jesus this afternoon and received him joyfully.' A boy of about twelve, he had slipped into the rear of the tent and been attracted by hearing his own unusual name, and the Holy Spirit had used a mothers'-meeting lesson given a year and a half ago to bring this boy to Christ.

"He was told to confess Christ at home. He went home, bringing his mother to the tent at night. She was converted. The third night he brought his aunt, and she was converted. Then a neighbor woman who had been interested before he was converted, but had refused to come into the tent, was brought by Zaccheus, and she too took Christ as her Saviour.

"But Zaccheus's father was incensed with the boy's confession of Christ, and when he refused to go for beer pounded him severely, and when his wife told him that she had accepted Christ as her personal Saviour, and that from this time on she would try to be a more loving, dutiful wife, he was aroused to all the furies of a demon. He cursed and abused his wife, who, to his surprise, took it silently and humbly, and then started for the tent with a pistol and knife to kill Mr. Williams and myself. Being prevented in this, he packed up his trunk and left home. He appeared to his wife one morning at nine o'clock crazy drunk, and was carried to the Washingtonian Home, but at half-past ten that night he was again at home. His wife was afraid to open the door, but, listening, recognized a sober man's voice instead of the drunken fury who went away from her. As she opened the door he fell into her arms and kissed her, telling her that he was a converted man. She awakened Zaccheus, and they had a prayer-meeting right on the spot.

"The aunt who had been converted lived in the same house as Zaccheus's parents, and she soon brought her husband under the sound of the gospel, when he was converted. Here, then, were the mother and father, aunt and uncle, and the neighbor—five grown people, in addi-

tion to the little boy—who were turned from the service
of Satan to God through the influence of that forgotten
passage in the children's meeting.

"But that is not all. The great burden on the heart of
one of the women was her unconverted fatherless brothers
and sisters in Nebraska. Sending a request to the mothers' meeting to pray for her, she started for Nebraska to
preach the gospel to them. Thus far her efforts have resulted in the conversion of one sister, and who shall tell
whereunto this thing shall grow?"

CHAPTER XXVII.

WITH THE GOSPEL WAGON.

VARIOUS methods were adopted by the evangelistic forces to bring the Word of God to the drifting crowds on the streets of the city, and to the men, women, and children who lingered about stores, saloons, and doorsteps in the evenings. One of the most effectual of these was the gospel wagon, which is really a small house and chapel on wheels, drawn by two horses, and admirably adapted for its purpose. The mission of the gospel wagon was twofold: to bring the gospel in short addresses and stirring songs to the ears of the people, and to advertise the various meetings in the theaters, halls, churches, and tents, to draw the crowds from the streets thither. The wagon was in charge of Evangelist J. C. Davis and the gospel singer H. I. Higgins. Other speakers and singers assisted, according to circumstances.

A visitor thus describes one of the services in which he participated: "A new and striking feature of the last week's work has been the gospel carriage. The strange vehicle has attracted considerable attention all over the city. Tuesday evening's work may serve as a sample. The carriage left the Institute about a quarter to eight o'clock and made for Townsend Street. When the destination was reached the carriage stopped close to the curb, a platform was hung out from the rear, a baby organ weighing only seventeen pounds set upon it, and a lantern hung out. The service was conducted by Mr. Davis and his singer. Several others assisted in the speaking and singing. There was a great throng around the carriage. The handsome appearance of the carriage and the comely dress of the speakers commanded respect, but what did more to hold attention was the vigorous, practical talking. No one spoke very long, and there was plenty of good singing."

Dr. A. J. Gordon, in an address upon the campaign, thus referred to this agency: "There have been two gospel wagons going about in different parts of the city dispensing the Word of life to such as may be induced to stop and listen, and the workers estimate that 1000 or more are thus reached daily of those who would not enter a church or mission hall. As I saw them one morning, they came up with a large furniture wagon, on which was a great placard bearing the words, 'Can the drunkard be saved?' Thus taking the most radical methods, the evangelists went about through the street attracting the gaze of the people. One of the workers took his stand in the midst of a great company of roughs and drunkards, and as they looked they said, 'What next?' Well, a great many of them came that night to find out if they could be saved."

The gospel wagon proved a good testing-place for speakers. If they could succeed there they could probably get along in other services. An eminent preacher from a Southern State, whose ministry had been confined to a large and fashionable congregation, one day ran the gauntlet of the street crowds on the gospel wagon, preaching four sermons from that wheeled pulpit. Speaking of that trip afterward, he said: "I have had a new experience today, in preaching to crowds of rough, dissolute, hardened men on the streets. I, who had been accustomed to a daintily carved pulpit, where the light came through stained glass windows, and where everything pleased the senses. I realized to-day, as never before, how Jesus must have felt as he preached to just such crowds of lost, wretched souls."

Another visitor who accompanied the gospel wagon one evening to a section of the city known as "Little Hell," on account of the fearful vileness, wickedness, and crime abounding there, says he was delighted to see even there "hundreds of orderly men and women with a host of little children gathered as close as they could crowd around the rear of the wagon, from which the platform is extended for the organ and speakers and leader of the singing, who only had to start some familiar gospel hymn to be followed by a full chorus of hundreds of voices, most of them among the children, evidently with Sunday-school training. So well did the little ones sing that when they came to the chorus the leader requested all the older ones to be silent and let the children sing the sweet words over and over again. As they did so, at the top of their childish voices, the well-known gong of the police-patrol wagon was heard ringing for its approach as the horses came at full speed, as the fire-engines go rushing along to a fire, but the crowd left room on the opposite side of the street, and the officers only checked their speed, without pausing, and passed by without molesting the meeting. Later on a policeman joined the audience and listened with the others."

One afternoon Mr. Moody mounted the gospel wagon and took command of what may appropriately be called the flying artillery of the evangelistic forces. His object evidently was to test that arm of the service. At his direction the wagon was driven through various sections of the city, and not less than ten different meetings were held in the course of a few hours. When a suitable place was reached the singers rang out a gospel song, then Mr.

Moody set the way of salvation before the gathering crowd in a five-minute address, gave them a cheery invitation to come to the evening service in the Standard Theater, then moved on to another place, where the same course was pursued, and so on to the end of the flying march. The experiment helped to confirm Mr. Moody in the conviction that the summer months offer the best opportunity to evangelize the cities, because at that season all classes, conditions, and beliefs can be reached in the open air, at their own doors, and the good news of salvation can be lovingly proclaimed in song and speech, and left to do its work. The gospel can thus be brought to many who need it most, and would probably not otherwise hear it, and many would be induced to accept the invitation to attend evening services in tents, theaters, halls, or churches.

One evening while the Scotch evangelist, W. Robertson of Edinburgh, was addressing a crowd of about 400 people from the platform of the gospel wagon, a tall, strong young working-man managed to creep beneath it for the purpose of overturning it. But the Spirit of God applied the word to his heart, so that at the close of the meeting he was under deep conviction and anxious to be saved. Taking him into the wagon, the evangelists dealt faithfully with him as they drove along; and while the following meeting was going on he cried for mercy and cast himself upon Christ for salvation. The following evening he was again present at the meeting, resting in the love of Jesus.

At the same service, when those who desired the prayers of God's people were requested to raise their hands, some persons responded in mockery and ridicule. Evangelist Davis warned them that although they might deceive him, they could not deceive God, and it was a solemn and awful thing to mock him. The rebuke was effective. A gentleman accompanied by a lady took off his hat and raised his hand for prayers. Two young men on the sidewalk had united in ridiculing the work all the evening. After a while, in response to the evangelist's appeal, one of them raised his hand; his companion took hold of his arm to draw him away, but in vain, and he finally left him and went away. Returning after a while, he again tried to take him off, with like result, and betook himself away. "You'll have no trouble to get rid of your evil companions," was Mr. Davis's pertinent comment upon the action. The onlooking multitude had thus before their eyes, on the open streets, successive object-lessons on the working of the Holy Spirit in the sinner's heart.

At the close of another meeting a young man, a visitor from New York, rushed forward, grasping Mr. Davis's hand, sobbing and crying out, "I do want to be saved. I want to become a Christian." After a season of instruction and prayer the evangelists had the joy of seeing the convicted soul accept Christ as Saviour and Lord.

CHAPTER XXVIII.

THE CHICAGO BIBLE INSTITUTE.

THE Chicago Bible Institute was the headquarters and central rallying-place of the working-forces by whom the World's Fair Evangelistic meetings were carried on. Mr. Moody has repeatedly declared that the Institute not only played a very important part in the work, but that it was essential to its success. In his address at the farewell meeting he said: "Little did we think, when we were praying, three or four years ago, to have a Bible Institute right close to this church, that we would have such an opportunity to preach the gospel to the world as we have had during the last six months. We would not have been able to do the work we have done during these past months if it had not been for the Institute, with its 300 workers gathered from every part of the country. Whenever we have started the work at any point we have had force enough to go right on with it. I think it would have been utterly impossible to have carried on this work without the Bible Institute to draw upon. Perhaps God raised it up for this very time, as Esther was raised up for the time of her people's peril and need."

Seeing that this institution has stood in such vital relations with the whole evangelistic movement in Chicago, some knowledge of its history and character is desirable in this connection. It was evidently born and ripened in the thought of Mr. Moody during his experience and observations in the fields of evangelism, as year by year he came in contact with the crying needs of the working-classes, the poor and the outcast, and the spiritual dearth in the great cities. He saw that a most blessed work could be done by men and women with knowledge and love of the Bible, and trained ability to use it in bringing others to Christ. The schools were not preparing such workers to meet the need. There was a call for an institution to offer the help which many consecrated but untrained young Christians desired.

The first step was to hold an institute in the Chicago Avenue Church, as an experiment and a test. Another and another followed, lasting from a few weeks up to three months, with surprisingly large attendance and encouraging results. The next step was an arrangement for organization of the work on a permanent basis. Land adjoining the Chicago Avenue Church was purchased, with buildings, which were fitted up for a Ladies' Department, and a building for the Men's Department was erected. At present there are accommodations in the buildings for over 300 students. The Institute began its regular work in October, 1889. The men's building was opened nearly four months later. From that time the work of the school has gone on without ceasing, with ever-increasing success and blessing.

The object which the Institute has set before it is concisely stated in the following terms:

"There is a great and increasing demand for men and women skilled in the knowledge and use of the Word of God, and familiar with aggressive methods of work, to act as pastors' assistants, city missionaries, general missionaries, Sunday-school missionaries, evangelists, Bible readers, superintendents of institutions, and in various other fields of Christian labor, at home and abroad. All over the land are those who would, with a little well-directed study, become efficient workers in these fields. There are also many men called of God into Christian work at too late a period of life to take a regular college and seminary course, but who would, with such an opportunity of study as the Institute affords, be qualified for great usefulness. There is a third class: persons who do not intend to devote their entire time to gospel work, but who desire a larger acquaintance with the Bible and methods of Christian effort, that while pursuing their secular callings they may also work, intelligently and successfully, in winning men to Christ. The object of the Institute is to meet the needs of these several classes. Besides these, many ministers and theological students, who have enjoyed the advantages of the regular training, have spent their vacations with us, getting a better knowledge of the English Bible, and how to use it in personal work, and a larger experience in aggressive methods of Christian service.

"The Bible Institute aims to send out men and women having six characteristics: thorough consecration; intense love for souls; a good knowledge of God's Word, and especially how to use it in leading men to Christ; willingness to 'endure hardness as good soldiers of Jesus Christ'; untiring energy; the baptism of the Holy Spirit."

"One great purpose we have in view in the Bible Institute," says Mr. Moody, "is to raise up men and women who will be willing to lay their lives alongside of the laboring-class and the poor, and bring the gospel to bear upon their lives."

The method of training is such as to realize most assuredly the object of the Institute. Study and work are happily combined. Theory and practice go together. A portion of several days each week is devoted to actual work in homes, cottage meetings, missions, tent meetings, and inquiry meetings, children's meetings, and industrial schools, the object being to teach students not only the theory of work, but also the work itself. The course of study includes : a comprehensive, systematic study of Bible doctrine; a general survey of all the books of the Bible; a close, analytical study of many books of the Bible; a thorough study of methods of winning men to Christ and building them up in Christian character; a careful and comprehensive study of all the different classes of persons that a Christian worker is likely to meet, and the Scripture to use in dealing with them; a careful study of vocal and instrumental music; and a development and deepening of the spiritual life of the student. Great emphasis is laid upon the latter.

The visitor who enters the Institute for a week's observation of its course of procedure and daily life will find something like the following: Monday is the free-and-easy day which the "boys" and "girls" call their rest day, when the usual daily order of study and work is laid aside. This Monday rest is needed the more because Sunday is always a time of service for the workers, and to some the busiest day of the seven. If the visitor is in the Men's Department he will be ready for breakfast on Tuesday morning at seven o'clock. At eight o'clock he will meet all the students in the prayer-room, where half an hour is devoted to praise and prayer. At nine o'clock both departments will assemble in the chapel to hear a Bible lecture, or to engage in class-room work, to which one hour is given. From ten to eleven o'clock is occupied in the study and practice of music, and lecture or class-room work fills the hour from eleven to twelve. At half-past twelve the visitor will be one of a crowd of hungry, hearty eaters at the dining-room tables. During the evan-

gelistic campaign the dinner hour was sometimes pushed
out to half-past one, on account of the noontide meetings
in the Central Music Hall.   In the afternoon the visitor
will find the students engaged in their various studies; or
going from house to house of certain districts, in course
of family visitation, where some of the best work is often
done; or taking some part in children's meetings and services of a similar character.   Supper at half-past five is
followed immediately by another prayer-meeting at six
o'clock.   Then the workers are sent out in detachments
to various mission meetings, numbering from fifteen to
twenty, which are held all the way from seven-thirty to
twelve o'clock at night.   Of course all do not stay from
half-past seven to twelve, but two different classes of
workers are engaged.   The program for every other day
of the week is practically the same as that of Tuesday,
with frequent evangelistic or other special services of various kinds, all bearing upon the one great object of the
school.

THE LADIES' DEPARTMENT of the Bible Institute, while
it is a part of the Institution—the "better half"—and in
study and work is one with the other department, yet oc-
cupies separate buildings, and has a distinct family life of
its own.   The well-behaved visitor who is so happy as
to be received into the gracious hospitality of this house
on a Saturday evening will have a little more time for
a morning nap than he would have in the Men's Department.   He will appear promptly at eight o'clock in one of
the four dining-rooms for breakfast.   Immediately after
breakfast, not on Sunday only, but every day of the seven,
he will enjoy a sweet season of devotion in the chapel,
with song, Bible reading, exposition, and prayer, conducted
either by the superintendent, her assistant, or some one
designated by her.   At nine o'clock four of the students

set out to conduct a morning service in the jail, and two others go to work in mission meetings. The rest of the students attend the services of various churches, according to their own preferences. Some of them have made it a part of their volunteer service to go out into "the highways and hedges," and with loving persuasion "compel" others "to come in" who would not otherwise attend church.

Immediately after the dinner hour four or five of the ladies go to teach in a Chinese Sunday-school. During the afternoon nearly all the students are engaged in some department of Sunday-school work, while some go on errands of love and mercy to the hospitals to read the Bible to the sick; others to hold religious services in houses where the sick, the aged, and the infirm cannot go out to church. In this work they have been greatly blessed, and no wonder, for it is just such work as makes glad the tender heart of the Son of God. Still other two students conduct services in two Homes of the Young Women's Christian Association. In the early evening two services are held in two of the police stations for the benefit of the police officers, two workers being assigned to each.

Daily evening devotions are conducted in turn by the students, who are expected to give a brief exposition of some portion of Scripture, and offer prayer. This service takes place in the dining-rooms, immediately after supper. For Sunday and Wednesday evenings a certain topic is previously given, on which each student is expected to contribute some lines of poetry for the Sunday evenings, and texts of Scripture on Wednesday evenings.

City missionary work is constantly being carried on, and not less than fifteen different missions, in various parts of the city, are receiving the benefit of the labors of these lady workers.

On Monday morning, which is the rest day for the Institute, the work of each student is arranged for the entire week, affording ample time and opportunity for necessary special preparation. As an illustration of such assignment of a week's work for the individual students we take the case of Miss B., who on Monday morning faces the following program: " Tuesday afternoon, conduct a children's meeting on Larrabee Street. Wednesday evening, attend a gospel meeting at Institute Hall. Thursday afternoon, street visitation. Friday evening, cottage meeting on the street. Saturday evening, home prayer-meeting." This program, of course, takes no account of the regular daily Bible and music studies of the Institute, to which reference has already been made, and which the students in both departments share alike.

The Ladies' Department is under the superintendency of Mrs. S. B. Capron, well and widely known as one of the missionary heroines of India, where she labored for thirty years with singular ability, devotion, and success. She came to the Institute enriched with the unpurchasable treasures of experience, thoroughly equipped in every respect for the place and the work that awaited her. After having been permitted to share the family life of this department of the Institute for several months during the evangelistic campaign, the writer has observed with growing admiration and satisfaction the admirable training and most gracious atmosphere and influence which are there enjoyed. In view of the fact that the young ladies of the Institute take their part in street work, house-to-house visitation, conducting services in police stations, halls, tents, and homes, coming in contact with the rough side of life, and all that, the anxious question has sometimes been asked, What is the effect of all this training upon them? Does it not make them bold, coarse, rude,

unwomanly? The answer is, It seems to work just the
other way. It seems to the writer that the gracious woman
who presides over the household, with her clear head, her
gentle, tactful, firm hand, her great, warm mother-heart,
her fulness of the divine life, is herself the corrective of
any such tendency, if it exists, and the security against it.
The atmosphere in which this Institute life and activity
unfold themselves is too pure and vital for such evil germs
to develop. There is here no encouragement for anything
to grow save that which is true and pure and of good
report. An English writer, referring to the department
"under the very genial and capable management of Mrs.
Capron," says: "She is a veritable mother in Israel, in the
highest sense of the term, and all who come under her
holy, kindly influence treasure it up as a very blessed
memory when the calls to work in many fields necessitate
the divergence of their paths. She also conducts a weekly
mothers' meeting, attended by some hundreds of women,
a vast number of whom can testify to the blessing God
had wrought in their lives through her teaching." It is
a rare privilege to listen to Mrs. Capron's expositions and
application of the Word of God in the daily morning hour
of devotion, in her Bible-class, and various other meetings
that she conducts. Here she gives free play to her keen
insight of truth and life, her deep knowledge of Scripture
in its interior, spiritual significance, happily combining
the wisdom of one taught in the school of experience
and the spiritual discernment of one deeply taught by
the Spirit of God. Many a devoted worker now in the
field, and many preparing to go from this Institute, will
never cease to be grateful to God for the ministry of Mrs.
Capron in the training for their life-work.

The following additional facts pertaining to the life and
work of the Ladies' Department have been furnished in

answer to a series of questions from the writer, by the hand of Mrs. Capron:

"Concerning the street work of the students it should be said that it is our custom to assign a certain section of some street of the city to an individual student; but two students usually go together in the work of visitation. Many a woman is found by these visitors hidden away in the midst of household cares, neglecting church and losing all care for better things. Such visits are greatly blessed. These mothers in the midst of their cares are encouraged to come to the Wednesday mothers' meeting held in the church adjoining the Institute. They can bring all their little ones, as these are cared for in the kindergarten room by ladies assigned to such work. There the weary mothers have a restful hour, and their souls are wakened to their deepest spiritual needs. Then they come to the Sunday afternoon Bible-class, the little ones being taken to the primary department in the adjoining rooms. They will then be inclined to attend the Sunday evening service of the church, and perhaps their husbands will join them. Then follows the Sunday morning service, and during all this the street visitor is doing her precious work in the home, leading to opening the room for a cottage meeting, it may be. Finally, we see these mothers enter the fold of the church. This is the history of many a woman who to-day says from a full heart: 'I do not know where I should have been but for the Institute workers.'

"All the students attend the classes for Bible study in the morning. Afternoons and evenings are devoted to practical work. Those who are out in the afternoon are expected to spend the evening in study, and evening workers have had the afternoon unbroken for the same purpose. Afternoon work consists in house-to-house visitation, conducting children's meetings, women's meetings, and calls for Sunday-school classes. Evening work is mainly devoted to gospel meetings and cottage meetings.

"The meeting for women, on Wednesday afternoon, is made up from women gathered from house visitation, with the workers on those streets, who are there to welcome them and introduce them to others. In this meeting a simple gospel teaching is followed by various testimonies from those women, not infrequently taking all the allotted time, the Institute workers being delighted listeners, especially when the speaker has been brought from the seclusion of an unblessed home. Some interesting meetings were the result of Gospel and New Testament distribution during the World's Fair evangelistic campaign. It was inspiring to see how the giving away a copy of the Gospel opened the mouth of the giver to speak some word of tender entreaty to accompany the gift.

"Five police stations are in charge of our workers, who conduct a brief service of singing, exposition of Scripture, and prayer, once a week, before roll-call.

"The sailors are not forgotten in the ministrations of the Institute. Hospitals also have their welcome visitors, and the children their special services.

"Soul-winning is the one object of the gospel meetings. There are many who have gone out to their life-work profoundly grateful for the privilege of having been in the Bible Institute, where they were enabled to obtain a clearer apprehension of the indwelling presence and power of the Holy Spirit, a practical knowledge of how to use the Bible in soul work, and helpful instruction in all the difficulties found in a work so filled with mystery, solemn responsibility, and inspiring hope.

"In all the various services of the evangelistic campaign conducted by Mr. Moody, the Woman's Department was well represented. The Ladies' Quartet was in demand at all the public services, in theaters, halls, tents, and churches. Indeed, all who could sing were in constant employ. In the after-meetings they were prompt, ready, and serviceable, and abundantly proved the value of their training. The Standard Theater meetings furnished many instances of conversions, and our students were always at home in the work carried on in the tents.

"It has been gratefully acknowledged that woman's work had a large share in the aggregate of the six months' campaign, especially in the song services, the after-meetings, the tent work, and the children's meetings. Miss B. B. Tyson of Washington, D. C., brought her invaluable aid in conducting not only meetings for children, in tents and halls, but her audiences on Sundays, composed largely of adults, were impressed and deeply moved by her clear, convincing teaching of the way of salvation, and many were led to Christ—men, women, and children. The value of her services cannot be estimated. Skilful and attractive as is her blackboard work, beyond that is the power within that comes only from the consciousness of being used by God."

In answer to further questions concerning the training of the students in the Institute, the following has been furnished by Miss Emily S. Strong, the devoted assistant superintendent, who thoroughly understands the life and work of the school:

"The training of the students is by no means limited to the Bible study or the practical Christian work, though these are large elements in it. The development of a symmetrical Christian character, the 'coming behind in *no* gift,' is the aim before those in charge for each student.

"The home is intended to be a *model* one in every smallest detail. Its spiritual atmosphere, so largely made and fostered by the wise and beloved mother at its head, is felt by all who spend any time here, and is responsible for changing the whole current of many a life. More than one has come hither young and immature, with crude ideas of Christian service, and little knowledge of the possibilities wrapped up in each redeemed soul, who, under the influences thrown around her, has gone out to fill a place of wide influence and large opportunity, and to fill it well.

"If there is one truth above all others which is emphasized, it is the doctrine of the Holy Spirit, as Guide, Teacher, and indwelling Friend, whose baptism is absolutely indispensable to fruitful Christian living and service. To many this has been new truth, which has opened up a wide field for study and meditation.

"One of the most helpful influences of the home life has been a weekly devotional meeting held every Saturday evening. Here the work for the past week is freely discussed, and the students come into closest sympathy with one another.

"A little midday service, where each student is sent out to her afternoon's work with a single precious thought from God's Word and a prayer, is also greatly valued by all in the home.

"In the students are represented every class of society, from those who have had every advantage of education and culture to those who can only claim a common-school education. It is surprising how all such distinctions are blended in a common family life, with one end and aim, all 'one in Christ Jesus.' Many come to us directly from their school life; others after some years of service, in which they have realized their great need of more knowledge of the Bible and methods of work. Some enter with very definite ideas of their future work. To others, the development of some latent gift often opens a field of labor unthought of before.

"Almost every State in the Union has had its representative here, and so each Protestant denomination. Since the Institute opened thirty-one women, or one out of every eleven, have entered the foreign work. Quite a number of returned missionaries also have been here, delighted with the opportunities for Bible study here afforded."

The Bible Institute began its work under the superintendency of Rev. R. A. Torrey, a man preëminently endowed and trained for the position, who still holds his place at its head. Under his capable hand, coöperating with its president, D. L. Moody, the Institute has been guided and developed along a course of phenomenal success, facing a future full of untold possibilities and promise. It has fairly won its distinguished place at the front of Christian training-schools, standing out among all other institutions with a distinct, strong individuality—a powerful Christian agency "come to the kingdom for such a time as this." Its brief history is a veritable romance of religious life and activity. It is the joy and delight of Mr. Moody's heart, for it is a power that works mightily for the highest ends of life, character, and destiny, to which his own life has been consecrated for years. In Mr. Torrey he has found a man after his own heart, who has thus far met every demand and responsibility of his position with the capacity and power of one called and anointed for his work. What Mr. Torrey himself thinks of the work in which he is engaged will appear from his answer to a question, when he said: "As to the Institute, I believe that there are few organizations on earth that will accomplish for the Church of Christ in the coming generation what this Institute will, in the way of winning souls, promoting Bible study, and increasing the spirituality of the Church. I consider myself one of the happiest, if not the happiest, of men, because of the privilege of being superintendent of the Institute."

During the World's Fair the Bible Institute, as the radiating center of the evangelistic movement then in progress, has been much observed and studied by thousands of Christian people, as a kind of Columbian exhibit of practical Christianity and gospel preaching and work for the masses. They have seen there in the masterly organization, with its song services, Bible teaching, and multiform Christian activities, a great object-lesson in aggressive work for Christ well worthy of their attention and study.

Nearly a year before the opening of the World's Fair arrangements were made by the London Polytechnic Institute, in conjunction with Mr. Moody, who was then in England, to organize a series of excursions to bring some fourteen hundred tourists to Chicago to see the Fair, who should have their home during their sojourn in the Bible Institute. This British host came on in detachments of one hundred each, following each other at intervals of a week. Thus while the primary object of these working-men was to visit the Fair, they had their headquarters amidst the best Christian influences and associations, and were brought in contact with an aggressive, religious, evangelistic life which could not fail to make its salutary impression.

But to no other class of visitors did their sojourn in the Institute mean more than to the teachers, preachers, evangelists, and other Christian workers who came and went during the six months' campaign. In addition to the many of this class who availed themselves of the summer's opportunity to study the Bible and prevalent methods of Christian work, Mr. Moody offered to entertain as his guests at the Institute the principals and teachers of his Northfield and Mount Hermon schools, to the number of about sixty.

It is worthy of grateful record that even a single day's careful study of the work and absorption of the spirit and life of the Bible Institute has been to some visiting ministers and teachers a revelation of possibilities in the direction of personal qualification and of aggressive Christian effort that will revolutionize their whole lives in the service of God. They have there seen, not beautiful theories and impossible ideals, but actual performance and realization. They have caught the inspiration of triumphant faith and courage, and have been enabled to go forth with the conviction that God is sufficient for all things, and that "what man has done, man can do."

The impression made upon the minds of veteran preachers by the Institute is indicated in such testimonies as the following: Dr. A. J. Gordon, the eminent preacher of Boston, in an address at Northfield, said, speaking of the evangelistic campaign: "Then the Institute work, I need hardly say, is the center of it all. I want to speak of this specially, for I was there giving Bible lectures each morning at nine o'clock. What surprised me in connection with that work was especially this: that room was filled at nine o'clock in the morning every day I was there; and mechanics, blacksmiths, and farmers were present in order to get the help for carrying on the work in the towns of the West from which they came. There were quite a large number of theological students present also, who had come to spend their vacations and take the lectures. I found not a few of returned missionaries present, and quite a number of pastors from different parts of the country who had come for the lectures, so we had from 350 to 400 listeners in the class-room of all these great varieties of attendants. Well, these men were frank enough to say: 'This is just what we want; we have had the minute study of Greek and Hebrew, but we want more biblical study. During July there were thirty-six preachers, evangelists, and singers and other agents coöperating in the work, and their labors were supplemented by an endless variety of house-to-house and highway-and-hedge effort by the two hundred and fifty students in residence in the Institute."

Evangelist Henry Varley of London, known and honored throughout the Christian world, writes to a London paper from Chicago: "The great central building where we all live and rally is the Bible Institute. I question whether the energy, ability, devotedness, and unity of hearts which exist here have ever been exceeded. As the waters in Ezekiel's vision flowed out, so here literally truth, zeal, and energy for God and man pour forth from nigh two hundred living springs. The impress of the beloved leader marks the majority of the students, and Mr. Moody appears to have engraved, under God, upon these young men and women who for more than four months have carried on this great and holy war, the motto, 'Out and out for Christ.' What a training for the gospel ministry!"

Mr. George E. Morgan, of the London *Christian*, after mingling with the students and entering into the life of the Institute, wrote to his paper: "One splendid characteristic of the students at the Bible Institute is their readiness to go at the word of command into church or slum, among poor or well-to-do, thieves or church-members, just wherever, at a moment's notice, they may be required. And a finer training for practical gospel work at home and abroad than is given at the Institute would be hard to find."

Rev. Hugh Montgomery, an able minister of Belfast,

Ireland, wrote from Chicago to the Belfast *Witness* a letter describing the evangelistic work and the Bible Institute, referring to the students as follows : " These two hundred and twenty young people are nearly all actively engaged in working up, for, and in the meetings. The young men distribute cards of invitation, visit the public-houses, beer-gardens, etc., etc., and come into personal contact with the very class which the special services are intended to reach. The young ladies sing in the choir, and help most efficiently in the inquiry meetings, as do also those of the young men who are not otherwise engaged. Mr. Moody has also a mission hall open nightly in the neighborhood of some of the large theaters. A number of the students live on these premises, come over to classes at the Institute daily, and then return to the hall and take part in the meeting which is held there. The lowest characters make their way into these gatherings. One of the young men who stood on the street to invite and urge the heedless hurrying crowd to come in was an Irishman. The rebuffs and raillery were all lost on him. He stood bravely by his post, and gave all and sundry a hearty invitation to the meeting. Gospel work in Chicago is almost literally 'pulling them out of the fire.' Sometimes a considerable part of an audience gathered in this way will be under the influence of drink, but, thank God, these brave young men 'keep pegging away,' and their fidelity and courage have been rewarded, for even there 'where Satan's seat is' have they seen that the gospel is God's power unto salvation. In the Bible Institute there are about twenty-five young Irishmen in training for Christian service. I had the pleasure of taking part in the good work with them, and of seeing the opportunities they had for aggressive Christian work. Will not those who read these lines pray that God may sustain and bless his servant Mr.

Moody? Those who can help him by their gifts will contribute to one of the most wisely and economically managed institutions in America. The officers of the Institute are all able and consecrated men, and those at the head of the Ladies' Department are no less able and consecrated."

As an illustration of how the leader of the evangelistic movement himself set an example of such service to the students, Dr. A. J. Gordon mentioned the following in an address on the campaign: "One thing I would like to say in Mr. Moody's absence. I think it is a true test, according to Jesus Christ it certainly is, of spiritual greatness, that one is ready to take any place. I was preaching one night in a hall in Chicago, on the first floor, where the people could flow in easily, and I looked through the open door and our friend Mr. Moody was out on the sidewalk pulling men in while I was preaching. He brought them in and seated them, sometimes taking hold of them and urging them with considerable energy to get them in; and that sort of service of pulling men out of the fire goes on repeatedly in that hall among the crowd of people, until two or three o'clock in the morning." [The hall referred to is in one of the worst places in the city.]

Rev. Mr. Torrey, in answer to a question concerning the summer's work, said: "The Institute played a very important part in the evangelistic campaign. In fact, Mr. Moody said the campaign would have been an impossibility if it had not been for the Institute. If he had to start meetings with short notice in any part of the city, the Institute made it possible for him to do so through the various students in a few moments. The printing for the work, the house-to-house visitation, the singing, the personal work in the after-meetings, and a very large part of the preaching, was done by the students of the Institute. The campaign was the experience and opportunity of a lifetime. The lives and work of all of us who had a part in the campaign will be different because of it."

In view of all that has been said, it is not surprising to read that "the superintendent is in constant receipt of requests for such workers as are sent out from the Institute. The only difficulty is to find men to supply the places. The demand so far exceeds the supply that men are hurrying to the work without adequate preparation, to the detriment of their whole future life and work."

CHAPTER XXIX.

THE LAST MONTH.

It was supposed that the meetings had reached high-water mark when on one Sunday in September about 64,000 people, in 70 different assemblies, listened to the Word of God. It could hardly be expected that the last month would surpass, or even equal, the more favorable preceding month. It was therefore with great joy and thankfulness that the still increasing interest of the meetings was observed. The second Sunday in October it was reported that about 72,000 people assembled in 109 different meetings, at 56 places of worship. And there would have been still more meetings if there had been more preachers and preaching-places available.

At the close of the following week Mr. Moody said: "We have to-day everything to encourage us, and nothing to discourage us. This has been by far the best week we have yet had. The gospel has through this agency been brought to 150,000 people during the week. I have never seen greater eagerness to hear the Word of God. The largest halls are too small for the crowds that come to many of the services. One night, for instance, on my way to a meeting held near the Fair grounds, I beheld one of the most beautiful sights I have ever seen on earth—that wonderful display of fireworks and illuminations. Tens of thousands of people gazed upon the scene. It seemed useless to expect anybody to come away from that scene and sit down in a tabernacle to hear the gospel. But the house was filled, and we had a blessed meeting. The following nights, though cold and rainy, with a damp, uncomfortable room, the people crowded in till every inch of space was occupied.

"I thank God that I am living in Chicago to-day. These have been the happiest months of my life. What a work he has given us to do! What encouragements he has given us! How he has blessed us! Probably never in your life will some of you have an opportunity to do as much for Christ as now. Improve the opportunity. Help us with your prayers, your efforts, your money. We are spending now about $800 a day in this work, and could spend $8,000 a day if we had it. We are getting new places for meetings as fast as we can. We want to press things in these closing days of the World's Fair as never before."

Cheering them On.

Deeply impressed with the greatness of the opportunity and the responsibility into which God's providence had opened the way, Mr. Moody's soul burned to make the utmost of the fast-flying days that yet remained. He urged his hearers everywhere to pray and labor with unremitting diligence. "It seems as if we had only been playing the past weeks," he said; "now we are going to work. We have just been fishing a little along the shore; now we are going to launch out into the deep. Friends, help to fill up the churches. Let us see whether we can't wake up this whole city. There is now before us the grandest opportunity of extending the kingdom of God that this country has ever seen. Hundreds of thousands of people will come in during these last weeks of the

World's Fair. It is possible to reach them with the gospel message. We want to get still more buildings for meetings near the Fair grounds. We'll hire all the theaters we can get. I'll use all the money you give me to push the work. Now is our time and opportunity."

On several occasions, in the Music Hall and theater meetings, Mr. Moody called for reinforcements to take part in the increasing work of the campaign. But he took care to let his hearers know just what kind of workers he was looking for. "We want more helpers," said he. "If there are any Christian young men under thirty years of age in the city, with good credentials, who will apply, we will give them work to do. If you don't like work, don't come. We don't want you. We want an army of workers to press this battle for Christ to the gate. If you come, there may be some things required that you don't like to do. If you are not ready for that, don't come. We've got to go out into the highways and hedges and bring the people in. I've got done building churches and waiting for people to come and fill them. What we want is to reach the people that don't come—the people that don't want to be reached. We want to raise up workers who will go for the people, instead of sitting down in churches waiting for them.

"Some of you have no idea of what is going on and what could be done. If I had fifty more good preachers and preaching-places, they could all be used to-day. I would to God we had five hundred earnest Christian workers in the Standard Theater alone every night. Hundreds of wretched, lost, despairing men could there be reached by such workers every night. Talk as you will about a future state and all that, I believe these men in their awful condition are going down to hell. If we don't rescue them they will perish forever. It is a question of life or death, of heaven or hell, with them now, and a few brief days will settle it. We have no time to lose.".

Words to Workers.

Realizing his own dependence on God, Mr. Moody constantly emphasized the necessity of divine help. He spoke again and again upon the work of the Holy Spirit, with special reference to efficiency in Christian service. On one memorable occasion he addressed a large company of preachers, evangelists, and other Christian workers, with subduing power. He insisted upon the indispensable necessity of spiritual power as a qualification for the worker, over and above all natural and acquired gifts and graces. He referred to his own experience, and said: "I would rather go to breaking stones on the road than to go into Christian work without the anointing of the Holy Spirit." He deprecated the graceless, powerless efforts of men to do a spiritual work without spiritual power.

"I believe," he said, "that there are more men turned against the gospel of Christ and against religion by workers who are trying to work for Christ without the energy and wisdom of the Spirit than in many other ways.

"There is no work on earth so glorious and sweet, so blessed and fruitful, as that of soul-saving. I believe God wants to make every one of us efficient workers, filled with his Spirit. He takes no pleasure in weakness, emptiness, and barrenness.

"When men are filled with the Spirit they will be ready for any work. They will not shirk the hard places and seek their own ease and comfort. They will not put the heaviest burdens upon others, but will lift them themselves. I know some men that I don't like to have around me. They are always looking for an easy job. They are good for nothing. They will soon be out. They will not be wanted.

"We must never forget that we are living in the dispensation of the Holy Spirit. The day we live in is his day. I was in the Church ten years before I knew anything especially about the Holy Spirit. When I heard a man in a noon meeting say that the Spirit was a person, and not simply an influence, I thought he was gone daft. I was amazed at it. But I took my Bible and read all that Christ said about the Spirit, and found to my amazement that it was even so. There is much of this ignorance still prevalent. We must know the Spirit of God if we would do the work of God. I do not believe we can accomplish much till we give him his proper place—give him right of way.

"It is the work of the Spirit of God to convict men of sin. We cannot do it by any amount of rhetoric, logic, eloquence, or human power. How often we hear of a man that he is cultured, learned, eloquent, persuasive, attractive, yet the people are not convinced and converted by his ministry. I verily believe that if the mighty angel Gabriel, who stands in the presence of God, were to come down from heaven into our churches, with every hair of his head blazing with the glory of that upper world, he could not convert a single sinner. Only the Spirit of God can do that, and he does it through the truth of God, preached by men filled with his power.

"Without the love of God no worker for God can succeed. It is the work of the Spirit to impart the love of God to the convicted heart. You cannot work yourself up to it. You cannot manufacture it. Do you remember how the love of God was shed abroad in your heart when you were converted? I see some of you smile. Ah, yes, you remember it. So do I. I was converted in a shoe-

store in Boston. Every time I go to Boston I go there.
It is still a shoe-store. When I want a pair of boots I
get them there. The place is memorable and sacred. I
remember when I went out of the store that day after my
conversion the world seemed a new creation. The air
was sweet and full of song. The sun lovingly kissed my
cheek. The breeze caressed me. Everything seemed new
and full of love. Ah, the Spirit of God had shed abroad
his love in my heart and made all things new to me.

"Without a spirit of hope and cheer no one ever accom-
plishes much. It is the Spirit that imparts hope. One
who is full of the Spirit is full of hope and cheer. If you
have lost hope out of your heart you had better get out
of the work, for you will only spoil it. Or, better than
that, you had better be filled with the Spirit, that hope
may revive. Cheer up, look up, lift up your heads!

"One who is filled with the Spirit works easily and with
delight for the Lord. The Spirit of God alone gives that
liberty that sets free all the powers of the soul for the
service of love. Men talk about overwork in the Lord's
service. I don't believe in it. It is overworry. That is
what frets and tears and wears out the worker. You
can't have that liberty without the Spirit. The work of
the Spirit in this world is to testify of Christ, the Saviour
of men. Now, mark: if you want the Spirit to work with
you and make your words effectual, you must proclaim
Christ, and not preach yourself, or your own notions or
theories. Otherwise, how can the Spirit work with you?
How can he testify of Christ in a sermon that has no
Christ set forth? What Chicago wants is to have the
Son of God lifted up, not men's thoughts, theories, science,
higher criticism, and all that.

"We must have the Holy Spirit to guide us into all
truth. This is his work. If we yield to him there is not

one necessary truth in the Bible that he will not lead us into. And all necessary truth for life and godliness is in that book. We get it only by revelation of the Spirit. He brings the words of Christ to remembrance. He lights up the words that lie cold and still in the memory and makes them live and speak and work in us. I verily believe that if the Holy Spirit had not come to men the very story of the life and death of Jesus Christ would have died out and been utterly forgotten from among men."

CHAPTER XXX.

On the night of Sunday, October 8, 1871, Mr. Moody, then a resident of Chicago, was preaching to a large congregation in Farwell Hall in that city. It was the fifth of a series of six sermons on the life of Christ, and he proposed to preach the sixth and the last of the series on the following Sunday. Even while he was holding up Christ to that congregation, that awful tempest of fire, which swept Chicago off the face of the earth, had already burst upon the city, and in a short time that congregation was a crowd of wildly fleeing fugitives, and their homes and the hall in which they had listened to Moody's appeals were heaps of smoking ruins.

The date of that most destructive conflagration in the history of the New World has been burned with flame into the memory of every Chicagoan of that awful, fateful time. The new Chicago resolved to celebrate the twenty-second anniversary of the fire on a colossal scale, hoping to draw the largest number of people to the World's Fair on that day that the city had ever seen. A "Chicago Day" celebration was accordingly announced, and Mr. Moody at once resolved to take advantage of the circumstances to make that eighth day of October, 1893, a great day for the cause of Jesus Christ. Arrangements were promptly made for an extraordinary meeting, with the entire force of evangelists and singers, from 10 A.M. to

184

2.30 P.M., in Central Music Hall. One part of the exercises was to be a repetition by Mr. Moody of the sermon he had preached on the night of the fire, twenty-two years before.

At the appointed time the immense hall was filled, with hundreds of disappointed people outside vainly trying to gain entrance. Four and a half hours the meeting continued without pause, rising to a climax of overwhelming power with Mr. Moody's sermon, which was given in the last half-hour. To the writer the service seemed not over an hour long, though eighteen songs were sung, solos, quartets, chorus, and congregational, with pipe-organ and cornet accompaniment, eight prayers were offered, and seven addresses were delivered.

"Will the people go and sit in a hall over four hours, to listen to songs and sermons, on such a perfect October day, when the World's Fair has put on all its glory?" This was the anxious question of many, who feared that Mr. Moody had made a mistake. The question was soon answered by a multitude of people that packed the immense building and overflowed into the street by hundreds. So great was the desire to enter that the doors had to be double barred, after the hall was full, to resist the pressure from without, and many went away with bitter disappointment who had come great distances to attend the meeting.

The writer, in order to gain a good point for outlook and hearing, climbed to one of the boxes hanging like birds' nests up near the dome. The scene was one not soon to be forgotten. There was an eagerness of desire, a hush of expectancy, that could be felt in the very atmosphere of the hall, as well as seen upon the thousands of upturned faces.

Now let us look and listen. On the platform are massed together the whole corps of evangelists, all the song-leaders, the quartets, and the chorus choir, with Mr. Moody at the front, like a veteran engineer on the engine of a "flyer," directing everything to its destined end.

The time has come to begin. "Let us sing 'All hail the power of Jesus' name,'" cries Mr. Moody, and the thundering organ, the two cornets, the choir, and the thousand-voiced congregation burst forth in a musical shout, "Let us crown him Lord of all." Surely this is worship! Surely there is heart and soul in this exultant song! "Let us all give thanks to God for his great goodness," says the leader reverently, and Evangelist Potter leads the worshipers in thanksgiving and praise.

Now another hymn, one of Moody's favorites, a metrical version of the one hundred and thirtieth Psalm, with the chorus, "For Jehovah I am waiting, and my hope is in his word," rings out in a mighty volume of sound. "Now let us all unite in prayer," says the leader, and Lord Kinnaird of London prays fervently, with thanksgiving and praise. "Sing Hymn 309, 'I shall be satisfied.'" Mr. Burke and Miss Hinton sing this beautiful song as a duet, while the author of the music, Mr. Stebbins, accompanies them on the organ.

"The Ladies' Quartet will sing." Four ladies of the Moody Bible Institute rise and sing "I will abide with thee."

"Let us unite in prayer." Dr. L. W. Munhall, of Philadelphia, leads the congregation to the throne of grace, and still the spirit of devotion rises.

"Let us sing Hymn 301, 'Saviour, lead me,' the congregation joining in the chorus." The choir sings these tender words, and the chorus swells out with the voices of the multitude.

"Mr. Towner will sing 'My Mother's Prayer.'" What a sweet, simple, pathetic song that is! See the people melting down under the song, as if they felt "the touch of a vanished hand," and heard "the sound of a voice that is still." Memories of far-off, sacred, happy days of vanished childhood, of home, of mother, come stealing through the souls of many. See that hard, sad, furrowed face softening, tears raining down over the cheeks. Poor man! he must have had a hard life of it since he broke away from the counsels and prayers of his mother. Gray-haired old men and women wipe their eyes and sob. Some men and women are trying hard to control their feelings, but they cannot hide their hearts altogether. The singer has touched "chords that vibrate once more."

"Let us again unite in prayer." Rev. John McNeill prays, and the worshipers rise with him on wings of faith before the face of God.

"Sing Hymn 135. All sing. If you can't sing, say 'Hallelujah.' You can all say that." How the people sing! The glorious "hallelujah" of the chorus makes the building thrill and tremble. It stirs Moody's soul. "Men tell us the Cross has lost its power," he cries; "does this look like it? Yesterday the gospel was preached to more people than on any day in the history of Chicago. Nothing draws like the uplifted Christ of the gospel."

"Now let us take up our offering. Help us to pay for the rent of the building. All give something." As the offering is being taken the instruments softly play the music of the hymn, "I need thee every hour."

"Mr. Varley will now speak to us. I call on him first, so that he can go over to the Woman's Temple and conduct a meeting there."

Evangelist Varley reads the account of the woman with a spirit of infirmity, whom Christ healed, and makes application of its lessons to Christians having life, but no liberty—bent, bowed, bound souls, who need the power

of Christ to loose them and make them upright. He
touches some of the great evils that afflict us. "I would
to God," he cries, "that you Americans would write down
and put down one of the worst institutions in your land,
the Sunday newspaper." "Hear, hear! Amen! Amen!"
the people respond.

"Mr. Jacobs will sing as a solo Hymn 101." The pleading song rings out sweetly from the singer's lips, "Jesus,
Saviour, pilot me," and amens are in our hearts.

"Let us sing Hymn 430. Let us all rise and sing."
Again and again the solemn question rings out in song
from thousands of lips, "When Jesus comes will he find
us watching?"

"Major Whittle will lead us in prayer. Let us all pray."
The major recalls past mercies, praises the faithful Lord,
and cries fervently to him for manifestations of saving
grace and power.

"The Ladies' Quartet will sing 'Rock of Ages,' a beautiful hymn." How sweetly these charming singers render
the dear old hymn, singing with grace in their hearts and
voices. The hymn and the music are favorites of Mr.
Moody, and he comments upon the song. "Do you know,"
he asks, "why this hymn is so sweet and precious? I'll
tell you: it is because the doctrine of the atonement is in
it. Oh, we cannot get along without that! It is what
this lost world needs."

"Mr. McNeill will now speak to us."

The Scotch preacher begins with a happy reference to
the dominant memory of the day. "I remember the time
when that tempest of flame swept over your city, and the
cry of her desolation sounded in our ears beyond the sea.
In that dark day God was your helper, and your sorrow
brought you near the hearts of the whole civilized world.
I don't know but that you were nearer God in that day of

your disaster and woe than now since you have waxed strong and mighty. In a conversation with Treasurer Harvey of your Relief Committee, he told me that the most touching gift he received was a box of clothes from one of the most destitute parts of destitute Ireland, poor, patched clothes of every description, in which Ireland is so rich. When you look upon your big dry-goods houses that reach up almost to heaven, it will be well to remember that box of patched clothes from poor Irish homes beyond the sea."

As a fitting key-note of praise for the day the speaker reads the opening verses of the one hundred and third Psalm. "The core of all praise is the throb and song of the heart. Oh, for the singing heart!" He opens the riches of the "inspired directory of praise," and evokes music from every sounding chord of the beautiful psalm. He closes with a vivid picture of the release and sunward flight of a captive eagle, the congregation breaking out in applause.

"Sing Hymn 348, 'His mercy flows an endless stream.' Sing as you never sung it before." And they do sing. Higher and higher swell the notes of the magnificent chorus. "Sing it again." And they sing it again and again. "Let the people on the floor of the hall sing it alone." The wave of song rolls over the auditorium. "Now let the first gallery try it." The chorus rolls up from the first gallery. "Now you people up in the second gallery sing it alone." Up in the dome, from the cloud of witnesses hanging over the auditorium, the glad chorus breaks out. "Once more! That was good." Again, louder, they sing it out with gladness and joy. "Now let everybody sing it." Everybody does. Organ, cornets, choirs, floor, stage, galleries, aisles, everything breaks out in the jubilant cry, "His mercy flows an endless stream, to all eternity the same." The waves of sound break upon my lofty aerie like the spray of a musical Niagara, and the dome rolls them back again upon the heads of the worshipers.

"Mr. Inglis will lead us in prayer. Let us all pray." The warm-hearted Englishman gives voice to the thoughts in our hearts, and soft ripples of "Amen" pass over the congregation.

"Miss Hinton will sing a solo, No. 116." Our thoughts are borne toward that happy time when "We shall meet our loved ones there, some sweet day, by and by," as she sings the beautiful strains.

"Major Whittle will now address us." The major is a Chicagoan. He recalls how he came to the city in 1857, and has made it his home city ever since. He also has his memorable experiences of the great fire burned in the memory. He recalls some of the incidents of the time, and makes spiritual application of them, centering all upon the supreme importance of the unseen and eternal things which abide when the glory and wealth of the earthly shall have passed away forever.

"Sing Hymn 318, 'Am I a soldier of the Cross?'" The familiar words seem to put on new meaning as they are rung forth under the inspiration of the hour.

"We will now be addressed by Dr. Pierson."

Dr. Pierson's stirring address has the glowing reflection of the great fire in all its parts. He relates some remarkable incidents of the awful conflagration that swept over the Northwest, which came to his knowledge in a journey over the wide waste of the burnt district, sixty by four miles in extent. He saw there a wooden church standing untouched and unscathed by the fire, a solitary monument in the desolation, with everything swept away by the flames around it. He preached in the church, and asked the people to explain the strange fact of the preservation of their church. They told him that the church had been built for them with money given for the purpose by a devout Scotch Covenanter. When the fire came sweeping down upon the settlement, the people fled for refuge from their homes to a ravine within sight of their church. There, with strong crying and tears, they prayed God to save the house built for his worship. Their own homes might go, but oh, let him spare their church! They looked as the mighty sea of flame came rolling on, devouring everything as it came, and to their joyful amazement they saw the flames parting asunder as they neared the church, and the red waves swept by on either side, licking up their homes, leaving the house of God without touch or smell of fire upon it!

The speaker proceeds to talk of the fire that shall try every man's work, and of the kind of work that shall abide the fiery test, concluding with an account of his own experience in the ministry, which issued in entire consecration and new spheres of blessed service in the kingdom of Christ.

"Let us pray. Mr. Needham will lead us in prayer." The evangelist speaks out of our hearts, and with one accord we wait at the throne of grace, receiving the blessings we seek.

"Let us sing." What! Nothing so fitting as the cry, "Nearer, my God, to thee," and oh, how the musical outcry of the throng rings out with heart and voice!

"We will have a word from Lord Kinnaird." The word which the British nobleman speaks is an appeal to the young to keep their record clear and clean, and an assurance to those who have failed that God can and will restore and remake that which they have marred, if they will but bring it to him.

"The Princeton Quartet will sing." The song is one of the most affecting and impressive yet heard in these meetings. It is the first seven verses of the twelfth chapter of Ecclesiastes, set to music that carries the sentiment irresistibly into the heart. One rarely sees a congregation solemnized, hushed, and moved as that touching cry of the ancient singer moves them.

"Mr. Munhall will now address us." In a rousing address the evangelist speaks of a current misconception of the fatherhood of God, and corrects it. He refers to nature's testimony to the wisdom, power, and glory of God, and shows that only in Jesus Christ can we find his saving grace and love declared and set forth. He speaks of the written Word as disclosing the living Word, and illustrates the power and sufficiency of the Word from the experiences of men, closing his inspiring address with a thrilling incident of the late Civil War.

"Hymn 74. Let us sing." It is two o'clock, and the hymn seems to be intended for the close of the meeting. It is "God be with you till we meet again." But now Mr. Moody rises to speak, and we are to have the promised sermon he preached twenty-two years ago, on the night of the fire.

It is a trying experience, for the speaker is profoundly moved, almost unable at times to command his voice or restrain his tears, as the memories of the past rush in upon his soul.

Following is a verbatim report of the sermon:

Mr. Moody's " Fire Sermon."

In the spring of '71, along with Philip Phillips and Rev. (now Bishop) J. H. Vincent, I went to California, and when I came back here hot weather had come, our audience had become scattered, and I came to Farwell Hall, wanting to get back the audience, but nearly all had gone, and it seemed almost impossible to get them together again. I remember that for a number of weeks I was turning over in my mind what to do to accomplish that. I thought I would get up some kind of sacred concerts, or get some one to lecture on historical events, for I thought that the gospel would not draw. But I remember that after praying over it and getting up from my knees the thought came to me, Preach to them upon Bible characters. Well, I had some six or eight Bible characters in my mind, and I thought I would try Adam first. So I took Adam and looked him over, but I thought I could never talk about him for thirty minutes. Then I thought I would try Enoch. I think I took up Noah next, and I came down to Abraham and had him as one of the characters. I advertised that I would speak so many nights on the Bible characters. It was not long before Farwell Hall began to fill up, and inside of five weeks I had the largest congregations I had ever spoken to in Chicago. When I came to Christ I intended to devote six nights to his life. I had been spending four Sabbath nights on the subject, and had followed him from the manger along through his life, to his arrest and trial, and on the fifth Sabbath night, the 8th of October, I was preaching to the largest congregation I had ever had in Chicago, quite elated with my success, having for my text the words: "What shall I do then with Jesus which is called the Christ?" That night I made one of the greatest mistakes of my life. After preaching—or talking, as I did not call it preaching then—with all the power that God had given me, urging Christ upon the people, I closed up the sermon and said, "I wish you would take this text home with you and turn it over in your minds during the week, and next Sabbath we will come to Calvary and the Cross, and we will decide what we will do with Jesus of Nazareth."

I have never seen that congregation since. I have hard work to keep back the tears here to-day. I have looked over this audience, and not a single one is here that I preached to that night. I have a great many old friends and am pretty well acquainted in Chicago, but twenty-two years have passed away, and I have not seen that congregation since, and I will never meet those people again until I meet them in another world. But I want to tell you of one lesson I learned that night, which I have never forgotten, and that is, when I preach to press Christ upon the people then and there, and try to bring them to a decision on the spot. I would rather have that right hand cut off than give an audience a week to decide what to do with Jesus. I have often been criticized, and people have said: "Moody, you seem to try to get people to decide all at once; why do you not give them time to consider?" I have asked God many times to forgive me for telling people that night to take a week to think it over, and if he spares my life I will never do it again. This audience will break up in a few moments and we will never meet again. There is something awfully solemn about a congregation like this!

You will notice that Pilate was just in the condition that my audience was that night, just the condition that you are in here to-day—he had to decide then and there what to do with Jesus. The thing was sprung upon him suddenly, although I do not think that Jesus Christ could have been a stranger to Pilate. I do not believe that he had preached in Judea for months, and also in Jerusalem, without Pilate hearing of his teaching. He must have heard of the sermons he had preached; he must have heard of the doctrines he taught; he must have heard of the wonderful parables that he uttered; he must have heard about the wonderful miracles that he had performed; he must have heard how Herod had taken the life of his forerunner by having him beheaded, and of the cruel way he had treated him, so that he was no stranger to Jesus of Nazareth.

But I do not believe that there is a child here to-day that has not a better knowledge of Christ than Pilate had. We have had more than eighteen hundred years of gospel proclamation in this dark world, and have seen the fruits of Christianity as Pilate never did. He never had seen Christ in his glorified state. The only time he saw him was in his humiliation, despised and rejected of men. The chief men that followed Christ were men of no account, men of no power, of no title, of no influence, of no position or culture. There was no crown upon his brow except the crown of thorns, no scepter in his hand except the reed placed there in derision and mockery. But we have seen Christ glorified, and we see him to-day by the throne of God, and we have far more light than Pilate had; and yet Pilate had his day; and I believe every man and woman have their day of opportunity. That was Pilate's day. The Son of God crossed his path that day, and he was exalted to heaven with privilege. It was a glorious privilege that he had. If he had decided according to his own conscience, even according to his own deceitful heart, and had been influenced by his wife, Pilate might have been immortal. He might have had his name associated with that of Joseph of Arimathea, with the twelve disciples of the Lamb, and with those foremost to herald the name of Jesus, if he had only acted according to his conscience. But there was another influence about him: the world came in, political preferment came in; the Roman government came in, and he wanted to win the favor of the Cæsars. There you see that weak, vacillating man in the balance, wavering. Hear his decision: "I find no fault in him."

Did you ever notice that God makes all his enemies testify that Jesus is the Son of God? The centurion who had charge of his execution smote his breast and said: "Certainly this was a righteous man." And Judas, after having betrayed the Son of God, said: "I have betrayed innocent blood." And Pilate had to testify that he could find no fault in him.

I do not believe that ever in the history of the world was there a more unjust judgment given than that of Pilate upon Jesus Christ. After examination he declared, "I find no fault in him," and in the same breath he said, "I will chastise him." The process of scourging was very cruel. They took the prisoner, bound his wrists and fastened him in a stooping posture, and the scourge, which is made of cord knotted with sharp pieces of steel, was brought down upon the bare back of the victim, lacerating the flesh, cutting it to the bone, and many a man died under the infliction. He scourged an innocent man, but he wanted to curry favor with the Jews and also hold with the Romans, and that was his decision. The Jews had the judge. They saw that he was vacillating, and knew that he was the man for them, and that they could get their own way. They said: "If you let that man go you are not Cæsar's friend." Then he tried to shift the responsibility. What man is there here who has not tried to shift responsibility in the same way? And I tell you that every one of you will have to decide for himself what he will do with Jesus; your wife cannot decide it for you; no friend on earth can decide for you.

It was the custom to release a prisoner at the feast of the Passover, so Pilate took the most noted criminal he

had and asked them whether he should release Barabbas
or Christ. He thought they would rather have Christ
than Barabbas, but they cried out: "Barabbas! Barabbas!" Then Pilate asked: "What shall I do then with
Jesus, who is called the Christ?" He had sent him to
Herod, but Herod had sent him back and refused to take
his life. And when he found that he could not prevail,
he was willing to go with the multitude, instead of standing up against the current.

What we want in this city is men to stand up for the
right; and even if you do suffer for a little while, the
crowning day is coming. We want men to stand up
against the current, not go with it; and not only to stand
up against the current, but to go right against it. There
was Pilate's failure. Would to God that he had had
the courage of Joseph of Arimathea! Hardly any name
in history shines brighter than that of Joseph. I can
imagine him that night in the council-chamber, when
Jesus was condemned by the sanhedrim. "What think
ye?" is the question. And then it rang out through the
judgment-hall, "He is guilty of death!" But away down
at the other end of the hall, Joseph arose, and with a
clear, ringing voice, he said: "I will never give my consent to that just man's death!" How that voice must
have refreshed the soul of the Son of God in that dark
night, when not one stood by him, when all cried out
against him! Oh, it is an honor to confess Christ!

There never will be a time when we can do more for
Christ than now, and there is no better place than here
in Chicago. May God help us to take our stand in these
dark days, when Christ is rejected by so many, and when
they are telling us that he is not the Saviour of the world,
and are putting him on a level with other men. Come
out and take a high stand for Christ. Let others go on

scoffing, but you come out and identify yourself with the disciples of Jesus Christ. Take a high stand—that is what we want to do. May God help you!

Pilate had come to the fork of the road. That was a memorable day in his history, for he had only to take the advice of his wife and obey his conscience. She had sent word to him, saying, "Have thou nothing to do with that just man; for I have suffered many things this day in a dream because of him." It may be that God warns you sometimes in dreams. He evidently did warn Pilate through the dream of his wife. I was reading not long ago of a mother who had a daughter who was away from home visiting with some friends. She dreamed that her daughter was murdered and buried under the barn floor. The dream made such an impression on her mind that she went and had the barn floor taken up, and there was the daughter just as she had dreamed. I do not know what Pilate's wife's dream was, but perhaps she had a dream of the judgment-day, and saw Christ sitting upon a throne with the angels about him, and her husband coming before him to be judged, and she was terrified and made haste and sent word to her husband: "Have nothing to do with that just man, for I have suffered many things in a dream because of him." Every man who had anything to do with the murder of Christ soon came to a terrible end. Be careful about your decision in regard to Jesus, for he is to be the Judge of the world.

I cannot detain you much longer, but I would like to-day to press upon you this one question: "What shall I do with Jesus Christ?" I cannot speak for the rest of you, but ever since that night of the great fire I have determined as long as God spares my life to make more of Christ than in the past. I thank God that he is a thousand times more to me to-day than he was twenty-two years ago. I made some vows after that Chicago fire, and I want to tell you that God has helped me to keep those vows. I am not what I wish I was, but I am a good deal better than I was when Chicago was on fire.

Just as I was preparing to leave London the last time I was there, I called upon a celebrated physician, who told me that my heart was weakening and that I had to let up on my work, that I had to be more careful of myself; and I was going home with the thought that I would not work quite so hard. I was on that ill-fated steamer, the *Spree*, and when the announcement came that the vessel was sinking and that there was no hope, and the stern sunk thirty feet, and we were there forty-eight hours in that helpless condition, no one on earth knew what I passed through during those hours, as I thought that my work was finished, that I would never again have the privilege of preaching the gospel of the Son of God. And on that dark night, the first night of the accident, I made a vow that if God would spare my life and bring me back to America, I would come back to Chicago and at this World's Fair preach the gospel with all the power that he would give me; and God has enabled me to keep that vow during the past five months. It seems as if I went to the very gates of heaven during those forty-eight hours on the sinking ship, and God permitted me to come back and preach Christ a little longer. And I would like to say that if there is a man or woman in this house to-day living under a broken vow, you had better right here and now, in the presence of these people, resolve to pay your vows before God. Sometimes we wait for a calamity to strike us. When the Chicago fire struck me I was in the middle of my life—if I live out the time allotted to man. After the fire I just looked around, and I cannot tell you what a blessing that fire was to me. I think when calam-

ity comes to us we ought to get all we can out of it, and
if God has a lesson for us to learn, let us take the lesson.
It may be that God has a wonderful lesson for us. I will
venture to say that many of you here have been in this
same state. You that are in the middle of life, look
around and ask yourself whether your life is what it
ought to be. Come to-day just for a little review, and
look down along the way from whence you came. Do
you not see some spot in your life where you have made
a vow and have not kept it? You have said, "I will be
a more consecrated man, or I will be a Christian;" you
have stood by the bedside of a dying mother and have
said, "I will meet you in the better world." Are you
going to make good that promise? Why not do so here,
just at the close of this four hours' meeting? Make up
your minds that you will carry out that vow. It may be
I am talking to a father or mother who has laid away a
little child. When that child was taken away you said:
"I am going to live a more consecrated life; I will not
get rooted and grounded in things below, but I will rather
set my affections on things above; I will make good my
vow."

It is only a little while, a few months, a few years, and
we will all be gone. May God help us now to pay our
vows in the presence of all the people. Come now while
I am speaking, and just make a full, complete, and un-
conditional surrender to God, and say, "Here am I, Lord;
take me and use me, let me have the privilege of being a
co-worker with thee," and there will be a fire kindled here
that will burn into eternity. This hour, this minute, make
up your minds that you are going to be from this time on
the Lord's side. Go to your home, to your church, and
give a ringing testimony for the Son of God. Go to work,
do what you can for Christ, and there will be grand days

for this Republic, and a blessed life for you here and hereafter.

With this closing appeal the speaker turns to God with a fervent prayer of thanksgiving, consecration, supplication, and tearful intercession for the city and for the multitudes coming up to the Fair. Then once more the people unite in singing, and are dismissed with the benediction, to meet again no more until all the earth shall stand before the judgment-seat of Christ.

CHAPTER XXXI.

THE last Sunday of the gospel meetings seemed like a hundredfold farewell service day, for it was manifest that the impression of the closing time was upon speakers and hearers. Every meeting seemed to be touched with the tender feeling of an approaching separation which deepened the solemn sense of responsibility. There was a great reluctance and an inward protest against the closing of the campaign. It seemed to many as if the movement so greatly honored of God should be continued as a part of the normal religious activities of the city; but it was clear to the mind of the leader that the extraordinary measures which had been devised to meet extraordinary conditions must cease, as they had begun, with them. Whether out of the experiences and impulses of the campaign a new crusade for Christ should hereafter spring forth, will be manifest in its time. Certain it is that the desire and demand for united, far-reaching, continued religious movements, commensurate with the greatness of the need, became increasingly apparent during the closing days of the World's Fair season.

Mr. Moody himself came to the last days of the laborious months with reluctance and regret. "I cannot tell you," he said to one of his congregations, "how sorry I am that this blessed work is coming to its close. This has been one of the most delightful experiences of my life.

202

I am so thankful that God has permitted us to preach the gospel to so many people during these six months. I think I have never had the privilege of speaking to so many Christian people as here. My desire and prayer is that they may catch the fire of God and carry it wherever they go. We expect that there will be results of blessing throughout the land and the world from these meetings."

Special efforts were made to press the work in the buildings adjoining the Fair grounds. In the Columbian Sunday-school Building, the Epworth Hotel Tabernacle, the Endeavor Hotel Tabernacle, the Vaudeville Theater, and elsewhere, strong forces of speakers, workers, and singers were concentrated. The suburban towns also enjoyed the ministry of some of the ablest men at command. Moody, Whittle, Dixon, McNeill, Wharton, Munhall, and others spoke with much effect. A remarkable feature of some of the meetings was the large proportion of ministers who attended them, aggregating as many as one thousand in one week. Results of conviction and conversion of sinners and quickening of believers were everywhere seen. The interest that had been so remarkably sustained throughout the long campaign continued to the end.

Last Meeting in Music Hall.

In accordance with Mr. Moody's original purpose the evangelistic campaign was brought to its close on the last day of the Fair, October 31st. The services of the day were a general rally in Central Music Hall for a continuous meeting from 10 A.M. to 3.30 P.M., as a conclusion of the great hall and theater meetings, and a final farewell meeting for the workers, in the Chicago Avenue Church, in the evening.

The all-day meeting, notwithstanding the special interest and attraction of the Fair on its closing day, was a continuous triumph, from first to last. The spacious building was not only full, and kept full throughout the entire service, but there was a constant overflow. About five hundred ministers had been specially invited, and there were probably never so many of the city pastors present at any one service. The entire force of evangelists and singers were on hand, ready to labor or to wait. Among those on the platform who took prominent part in the meeting were: Mr. Moody, who presided, Rev. John McNeill, Dr. O. P. Gifford, Rev. R. A. Torrey, Rev. John Williamson, Dr. Leech, Mr. Charles Inglis, Rev. W. A. Phillips, Dr. F. A. Noble, Dr. Mandeville, Dr. E. P. Goodwin, Rev. Joseph Cook, L. W. Munhall, Evangelist Brown, Henry Varley, and the song leaders, Towner, Burke, Jacobs, McGranahan, Chess Birch, and others.

Promptly at ten o'clock Mr. Moody rose before the eager, expectant multitude to open the exercises, and three thousand voices, led by Professor Towner, and supported by the great pipe organ and two cornets, made "a joyful noise unto the Lord." Then followed prayers, and songs by soloists, quartets, chorus choir, and congregation, and addresses, without pause or intermission, until the closing moment. Eighteen hymns, nine prayers, eleven addresses, with pertinent remarks and comments by the chairman, filled the hours with interest and blessing.

Speakers and Speeches.

The prominent city pastors, of various denominations, and other speakers, who made addresses, spoke in strong terms of generous recognition and hearty appreciation of the good results of the evangelistic work done during the campaign.

Rev. W. A. Phillips, of the Methodist Episcopal Church, in a stirring address expressed his conviction that the movement had already proved a great blessing to this city, this country, and indeed the whole civilized world. "On the part of my own congregation," said he, "I can say that we stand covenanted with this man of God, Mr. Moody, to press this work of soul rescue."

Dr. F. A. Noble, of the Congregational Church, spoke of the great achievements that the past six months have witnessed in Chicago; "but," said he, "the boldest and most successful thing that has been accomplished is this marvelous series of meetings organized and carried on by Mr. Moody." Of these meetings, among other things, he said: "They have been greatly helpful to the churches. We would not have realized in our churches and Sunday-schools this summer what we have, had it not been for this magnificent series of meetings. They have also demonstrated the exceedingly important fact that what the people want is the old, old story."

Dr. Joseph Cook, of Boston, testified his confidence that the unadulterated gospel of Jesus Christ had been preached in the city during these meetings, and therefore the usual signs of salvation from sin followed.

Dr. O. P. Gifford, of the Baptist Church, spoke most appreciatively of the effect and influence of the campaign. Said he: "The Christian pastors of this city looked forward to the World's Fair with anxiety and apprehension, fearing that the churches would have to call a halt of their Christian activity during the season. As pastors we cried to God. The answer that came to our prayer from God was D. L. Moody, and we were not disobedient to the heavenly vision. The result has been a magnificent triumph of the gospel and a real upbuilding of the churches, but especially a wide-reaching influence throughout this and other lands."

Dr. E. P. Goodwin, of the Congregational Church, said that he had for the first time in twenty-six years of ministry spent his entire summer in Chicago, and he did it for the sake of these meetings. He testified to the manifested power of the old gospel, preached in all simplicity, to attract and hold the great multitudes that thronged to hear it, and to save all classes and conditions that accepted it. "The thing that impressed me," said he, "was that there is a way to reach the people. I have seen it in the theater meetings, where the lowest and the vilest thronged to hear the gospel and were brought to Christ. God be praised for these brethren and for this summer's work."

Dr. L. W. Munhall, of Philadelphia, said that when he first learned of Mr. Moody's purpose to conduct evangelistic meetings in Chicago during the World's Fair he concluded that, for once, the evangelist had made a mistake. But the event has proved otherwise. "Surely the work has been of God, and has been a great blessing to the churches of this city as well as to multitudes throughout America and Europe."

All the speakers named spoke at some length, some of them also on themes suggested by current events, such as the assassination of Mayor Harrison, on the preceding night, and the munificence of a Chicago millionaire, with application of Christian principles. Rev. John McNeill spoke in the early part of the meeting, then went to Willard Hall to address an overflow meeting. Mr. Moody introduced him with an affectionate reference that touched a tender chord in many hearts. "This dear man," said he, "has stood beside me through all these meetings. I have learned to love him. He is very close to me. He is going away from us now. This is his last day among us. May God bless him in his work beyond the sea." Mr. McNeill dwelt principally on faith in Christian life and work. "God," said he, "has given to us in this campaign a splendid triumph and reward of faith. The difficulties seemed to be enormous, but God laughs at difficulties and impossibilities."

Mr. Henry Varley expressed his joy in having been permitted to labor with Mr. Moody in this great movement. He spoke especially of the Christian as being led in triumph by God, redeemed, accepted, glorified.

Mr. Charles Inglis portrayed the heroic Gideon as an example of faith in fellowship, worship, and work.

Mr. Moody spoke of the necessity of Christian assurance, real communion with God, loyal devotion to Jesus Christ as Lord, and singleness and concentration of purpose in life and work.

Rev. R. A. Torrey made the closing address. He said in substance: "We look over this audience this afternoon and see something over two thousand followers of Jesus Christ. What would be the result if these two thousand went out of this hall to win souls for Christ? We have talked and listened here, but if we should rise to-day and go out of Music Hall to all parts of this nation to win souls for Jesus Christ, we should see the greatest revival and the greatest victory for our Lord that this world has ever seen.

"There are some of us to-day who desire to shine down here, but if we could do it, it would not be worth the while. The brightest star in the financial firmament twelve months ago has passed away. The brightest star in the political heavens died out in clouds and sadness. Last Saturday night the brightest star in Chicago politics was quenched by an assassin's revolver. Friends, it is not worth while to shine down here, if we can but shine up there.

"I wish to make one point here: how can we all be

soul-winners? I answer, by being converted ourselves.
The man trying to hold the world with one hand and
Christ with the other will never be a soul-winner. The
next thing is that we be emptied of our own strength.
Then we must also understand the Word of God. And
we must be much in prayer. To have power with men
we must have power with God. I believe the great reason of the Church's weakness to-day is the lack of power
with God. There was never a time when we had so many
wise methods, but there is the one fatal lack of power
with God. The reason of that lack is, we do not lie on
our faces before God enough. Dr. Stephen Tyng, when
dying, said, 'I do not wish I had preached more; I do not
wish I had worked harder; but I do wish I had prayed
more.' We must believe that we have a prayer-hearing
and prayer-answering God. And, once more, we must
have the baptism of the Holy Spirit. This doctrine is
coming to the front. Power by the Spirit. We are
plainly told in Peter's sermon on the day of Pentecost
how we can obtain that power. Everybody can receive
it. If we ask and claim the great gift we will all go forth
clothed with power to work for God as we have never
worked before."

With prayer, song, and benediction the five and a half
hours' continuous service came to its close. But still the
people lingered in the hall, as if loath to leave for the last
time the place where so often the grace and power of God
had been made manifest during the memorable weeks and
months now passed away.

The Farewell Meeting.

The place fitly chosen for this final and farewell service
was the Chicago Avenue Church, where the first services

inaugurating the movement had taken place, six months before. The church was filled at an early hour with a congregation such as will never again be seen there. Seats, stairways, and standing-room were occupied. Mr. Moody presided. A prelude of song befitting the occasion was conducted by Mr. D. B. Towner, in which other song leaders, quartets, and choir, as well as congregation, took part.

Evangelist Charles Inglis of London was called upon for a parting message, and addressed himself with deep feeling and pleading words to the unsaved, inviting them to respond to the loving call of Jesus and accept salvation at his hands. To his co-laborers he said: "I confess, dear friends, that there is always a tinge of sadness about last meetings, and especially about our meeting to-night. You shall never gather again in this city as we have been doing in our Master's service, for the ranks are beginning to thin, the standard-bearers are going. But it is a joy to remember that we shall meet yonder, in the morning, where we shall see the face of our blessed Master and dwell in his presence forever. God bless you! Amen."

Mr. Moody's Address.

After singing another hymn Mr. Moody spoke as follows: "I want to read to you Esther iv. 14: 'For if thou altogether holdest thy peace at this time, then shall there enlargement and deliverance arise to the Jews from another place; but thou and thy father's house shall be destroyed: and who knoweth whether thou art come to the kingdom for such a time as this?' Little did we think when we were praying three or four years ago to have the Institute right close to this church that we would have

such an opportunity to preach the gospel to the world as
we have had during the last six months. We would not
have been able to do the work that we have done during
the last six months if it had not been for the Institute,
with its three hundred workers gathered from every part
of the country. Whenever we have started the work at
any point we have had force enough to go right in and
give it a good start. I think it would have been utterly
impossible to have carried on this work without the Bible
Institute. Perhaps God raised it up for this very time,
as Esther was raised up for the time of her people's peril
and need.

"When we commenced this work six months ago it was
with some fears. The question was, Could we reach the
people who were coming up to attend the World's Fair?
Would they have the time or any heart for religious services? The impression was that they would be under
such heavy expenses that they would rush right through
the city, and we would not get a chance to speak to them.
But God has outdone all our expectation. The great
trouble has been with ourselves. To-day we should have
had every theater. Instead of having only the Music Hall
and the Willard Hall, we should have had them all. I
have upbraided myself all the afternoon that I was so
stupid. God has gone away beyond our faith. When
the financial crash came and men began to be troubled, I
did not know where the money was coming from to carry
on the work, and one day I was quite cast down, when a
despatch came from the little town of Northfield which
said they were sending ten thousand dollars. It looked
as if it had come out of the ground. Our account at the
bank has been overdrawn three thousand dollars, but the
money has come; I do not know where it has come from;
I cannot tell you; but it has come. The flour barrel has

been pretty near empty every now and then, but the flour has kept coming.

"It is remarkable, too, what weather we have had during the last six months. We have had hardly any rain. It rained one Sunday morning, but it cleared off so that we did not have to use an umbrella. I had some fears about cholera; but I said, If we do have it we cannot run, we will face it; but thank God, we have had no disease. Death has been kept away from our workers, and every man and woman has kept at work. In fact, the Lord has been better to us than we deserve; we cannot praise him enough.

"And what a grand privilege we have had to preach the gospel, not only to our own great Republic, but to the nations of the earth. And I believe down deep in my heart that the best six months that Chicago has ever seen have been the last six months. There has been some disappointment; the whisky men have not sold as much whisky as they expected, and a great many of them are very much disappointed. I thank God that their business suffered. I pray God to bless them, every one, and smash up their business. I believe there is something better than selling whisky, and I wish every man of them out of it. I want to say that I believe firmly that if the Church of God would unite and pray and work we would smash up the whisky business. We want to close up the whisky shops of Chicago. If prayer kept people from going to the World's Fair on Sunday, let us believe that God can keep people from going to the whisky shops.

"I want to say that things look brighter to-night than they did six months ago, when we came into this church and set the work in motion; and it has spread not only over the city, but over the nation. God has been with us; the shout has been heard in the camp for the last six

months. I praise God with all my heart for the band of
workers that has been sent us—from Australia, from
France, from Germany, from Scotland, from Ireland, from
England, and every city in this Republic. I thank God
we have worked in perfect harmony—Baptists, Methodists,
Presbyterians, Congregationalists, Lutherans, and I don't
know what—we are all mixed up—I do not know what
we are! I do hope that you Christian people here in Chicago will just take up the work and hang right on to it.

"Before I forget it, I want to say that any of you Christian young men can get a room free of rent, right along
through the winter, if you want to give your nights to
Christian work. And if you want to give your whole life
to Christian work, you can find out whether you have any
fitness for it. I believe that hundreds of men have got a
gift for the work, and do not know that it is in them. It
has to be brought to light. I do not think a man at the
age of twenty can tell what he can do for God until he is
tested in the work. Some men are always coming around
asking me what I think they ought to be. I cannot tell
what your gifts are. We started this Institute to develop
and show what they were fitted for. If you are adapted
to house-to-house work, you will find it out; if you are
adapted to visiting the sick, you will find it out; if you are
adapted to going into the byways and hedges, to speaking
on the streets; if you are adapted to evangelistic work—
you can find it out after being in the Institute about six
months. Here is a pretty good opportunity for some of
you young men here to put your winter evenings into
Christian work. I will tell you that if God does call you
into this work, you could not go into a better business.
The greatest struggle I ever had in this city was as to
whether I should give up business and go into Christian
work. I thought selling boots and shoes the most impor-

tant thing; but, thank God, I have put the world under my feet, business and everything else! And I have never seen a moment since God took me out of business that I ever regretted it.

"If God opens the door for you, you go in. What would Moses have lost if he had not gone to Egypt when God called him! What would Elijah have lost if he had not gone to Horeb when God called him! What would Daniel have lost if he had not taken a stand when he went into Babylon! My friends, take your stand for God and say, Here, Lord, if you want me to go into your work, I am ready, and if you want me to stay in business, I am ready."

McNeill's Farewell Sermon.

After Mr. Towner and Mr. Burke had each sung a solo, and Mr. Moody had led in prayer, the Rev. John McNeill was introduced and proceeded to preach the sermon of the evening, which was to be also his farewell message to Chicago, after his long, faithful, effective labors in the city. "I remember," said he, "the night that I stood here, six months ago. I had a little feeling of homesickness; but I have a different feeling to-night in looking back. How God has kept and sustained and blessed us! I said in the Music Hall to-day, and I feel it to-night again—I am not good at making farewell speeches, and I am not going to try. And yet I want to say just a word as to how glad and thankful I am that I was permitted to come and bear a small part in God's work here. There have been difficulties and trials, and I have been made to feel that if it had not been the Lord's work I would not have stuck in; but it is the Lord's work. He has graciously manifested himself among us, opened doors for us, and given us health and strength to enter in. I have been longing to be back on the other side; but it would have been a positive sin, as well as weakness, if I had allowed it to draw me away from such a Master and such co-workers."

With these and other preliminary words the speaker came to the theme of his sermon, "Working out salvation," based on Philippians ii. 12. "Paul," said he, "had been working among the Philippians, as Moody and the rest of us have been working among the people of Chicago and the World's Fair people, and after working for a while he passed off and wrote a letter back. He seems to have heard that these Philippians were very fond of him and were missing him, and they were saying to themselves that it seemed to be easier to believe, and easier to live the life of faith, to resist one's own rebellious flesh, and fight the battle of temptation and sin when Paul was with them. But now Paul is away, and there is a kind of dulness and heaviness and faintness coming in. 'Wherefore, my beloved,' he said, 'not as in my presence only, but much more in my absence, work out your own salvation.' Not hanging hands and trembling knees, but 'much more,' now that we are separated. It has been a blessed time in Chicago, but let none of us, now that it is over, hang our heads and sorrow and mourn. It has been blessed to be here, but it is blessed all the way. The Lord is always with us. Moody passes on; Varley passes on; Munhall passes on; McNeill passes on; but 'it is God that worketh in you to will and to do of his good pleasure.' We part in God's name; we met in God's name; and we will meet again in God's name. What blessed service it is while we are together, while we are in each other's presence as we are to-night, though we soon part. What a blessed service is the service of Christ—what a glorious opportunity to talk of him daily! How sweet to preach and pray and unite in praise and worship in speaking and hearing!

How rapidly the working-hours in these days of service pass! How rapidly the closing hour, the time of rest, draws nigh, when all the faithful shall be gathered home, a joyful company, home where the Master is, and see his blessed servants! Paul and his Philippians have long ago met to part no more. This is in store for Moody and all of us in this campaign. Now, then, the Lord's command is upon each of us, that 'much more,' in each other's absence, we should 'work out our salvation with fear and trembling.'

"I sometimes think that this verse receives its fullest emphasis by taking it from Paul's mouth and putting it into Christ's. We hear it as coming not from Paul the servant, but from Christ the great Master within the veil as he looks down on us, speaking to our hearts, 'Wherefore, my beloved, not as in my presence only, but now much more in my absence, work out your own salvation with fear and trembling; for I have disappeared from your eye, but I am reappearing in your hearts, I am working in you to will and to do my good pleasure.' You have not seen Jesus, because Jesus is not here in the flesh; but it is expedient for us that he be away, therefore in God's name let us be up and at it; not less, but more, because Christ's person is removed from us, let us realize Christ's presence within us, the spring and energy for life and godliness, until he shall appear and faith be lost in sight.

"Now, just a word to somebody here who may be in a puzzle about this text. . I can imagine some man here saying, 'McNeill, what about that text, "Work out your own salvation"?' Well, my friend, what are you going to do? Perhaps you mean that this text denies that salvation is a work of God? There is no such thing taught in the Bible. Salvation needs to become your own. Unless you

take salvation as a free gift from the hand with the nail-
hole in it, you are not saved yet, and it is about time you
knew it; and you had better be saved just as quickly as
you can. A salvation not by works, but a salvation by
simple faith in Jesus Christ, is the best kind of a salvation
for a Chicago man; isn't it? The quickest salvation is
the best; and there is only one salvation: the salvation
summed up in two words, 'come' and 'take'—God gives
and I take. Then I am ready for anything. You may
fill me with bullets if I have accepted Christ's salvation;
you simply do me a good turn, you send me home. You
try to kill a Christian, try to spite a saved man, a man
trusting as a poor sinner everything to Christ Jesus—it
is very much like trying to spite a ship by launching it.
A ship, although built on the land, is meant for the ocean;
and the believer, although he begins down here, is meant
for heaven, and blessed is the instrument or shot that
sends him to his true and eternal home. Take God's salvation as a free gift, and it is your own; then work out
your own salvation. All you do is to take it as a free
gift, and then it is your own; then you can work it out.

"I have nothing that I can call my own but my sin and
my guilt, my wretchedness and my misery. That is the
only thing that is my own. Is my property my own? A
man walks abroad to-day and says, 'This is my property,
this is my own;' and that very night there is a fire, and
his property goes up in a fiery chariot and comes down in
a shower of soot. How can that be if you can call your
property your own? Another man says, 'My wealth is
my own. See that pile—that is mine.' But a man's
wealth is not his own in any real sense of possession.
The bank breaks, and where is your money? Riches take
to themselves wings and fly away, and they do not leave
any message as to where they went. My own! My wife

my own! Sure, that is your own. But how uncertain it
is! Some day he walks broken-hearted behind her coffin.
How does that happen, if I can say 'my own' in any
real sense of possession? My friend is mine; but who
has not lost his friend? I am coming closer. My own,
my first-born child—a new, complete baby—the latest
thing in babies! And the happy mother says, 'Surely
this is my own.' But while she hugs her first-born baby,
that mysterious power called death comes in between the
babe and the bosom, and hug it as she may, she loses her
treasure. She has at last to bury her dead out of her
sight.

"But to return to my text—my own salvation. Hear
that, devil! My own salvation! The thing which by
nature I have no right or title to. Blessed be God, it is
the only thing that is absolutely my own! My own salvation—that the grip of death shall not unclasp. Death
will only give Jesus and the believer completely and finally
to each other. My own salvation, because it is a free gift,
a gift from God. And when God gives it he will never
take it back. Accept salvation as God offers it. The
gift of God is eternal life. Take it, and then you are
ready for my text, 'Work out your own salvation.' But
until it is your own you cannot make anything out of
Paul's injunction. After accepting salvation as a free gift
from God, I discover that I am in for it. I am gloriously
in for it. That is the gift you are to work out. It is the
only gift that will work out. The moment I accept Jesus
Christ, God's gift to my guilty, perishing soul, I will work
it out. Many a gift will not 'work out.' Let me give
an illustration: there is a gift that some people get—a
beautiful clock. Ministers often get clocks from their
congregation. I never got one yet, but no doubt it is
coming. The deacon or the elder presents the gift, and

the minister is so pleased that he turns everything upside down. He does not value it for its cost or its workmanship, but for what it represents—love and affection. There seems to be a halo around about it. That is what gives it its value. I can imagine the minister and his wife gathered around the clock as it stands on the mantelpiece. His wife says it is such a lovely thing; she rubs her hands as she looks at it. Lovely! gold and silver and filigree work. It tells the days of the month; it tells the month; it tells the weather; very fine; but it does not always tell you what o'clock it is. But there it stands, and it works out. But the best gifts stop; they come to an end. Children will get sick, and the husband and wife will not think to stand before that gift-clock and get encouragement. The clock will come to a dead stand, and maybe the minister and his congregation will begin to differ by and by. The gift will work out no more. It comes to an end. And all earthly gifts, at the best, come to an end. But this salvation will work out and expand every day you live, and the more you draw upon it the fuller it becomes. 'Work out your own salvation.' Oh, what a gift Christ is!

"There is a poor miserable backslider. You have not exhausted the unsearchable riches of Christ. They would not be unsearchable if you could. Come back to Christ, and you will find him as full to-night as ever. Why did you ever play the fool and leave? You say you have a bad temper. I am glad you admit it. Do you mean it, now? But work out your own salvation from bad temper. The quicker the better. You say you have a secret lust that roars at you like a lion; but it is in the grace of Jesus Christ to break the very lion's strength. 'Work out your own salvation.'

"Now let us get on to the command, '*Work out* your

own salvation with fear and trembling.' That is what I
wanted to get at. You have to be active. God's sover-
eignty and power evoke human responsibility and activity.
You have it, therefore work it out. To use a common
illustration : there is a load of bricks here, a load of timber, and some slates. That is not a house. No; but there
is the making of one, and you can make the house out of
it. Now the Lord lays all down at our door; he puts it
into our hearts; he comes with the plan and the specifica-
tion and the material, and says, 'Now work them out.'
Rise to the work; you have got to build a temple for your
God, and a house for yourself in which to live and dwell
forever; you have to build a spiritual house; you have
got to raise in your character and life a spiritual fabric,
a copy of the Lord Jesus Christ—work out this business.
The Greek has at its root the idea of 'energy.' Oh, what
a pulsing word—*energize* your own salvation. Now there
are just a number of people needing the word 'energize.'
The doctrines are lying on your souls like great unwrought
lumps of dough that you have not worked out—I speak
to housewives—and no man can feed on dough; it will
kill him ! Many of you are dyspeptics, feeding on gospel
doctrine that you have not kneaded and fired—and I don't
know what—but you understand what I mean ! 'Work
out your own salvation.' Get up now, put your feet below you, fling off your coat, turn up your sleeves, and go
at this business like the work of a lifetime, and never stop
it, this work of saving yourself, if I may be as contradic-
tory as the Bible is. What a work needs to be done !
When the Lord comes to me in all the light of his saving
grace he shows me what to do. He brings all with him
that is needed; but I am not to be lazy; I am not to lie
back and do nothing. There is a kind of teaching of the
'higher life' abroad, and I do not say a word against

higher life if it means being holier and working out your own salvation more diligently. But there is a kind of teaching abroad that is too passive. Its favorite illustration of the fact that you are in Christ, and Christ is in you, is the sponge. The sponge is in the sea, and the sea is in the sponge, and there you are. There you may be, but I prefer to come here. 'Work out your own salvation with fear and trembling.' *Work*, because, as the text shall afterward show, you are not working in your own strength; behind all your energies there is this eternal mainspring that enables you to work easily, swiftly, without friction, and without failure—'God worketh in you to will and to do of his good pleasure.'

"Now you know what to do. You have a bad temper —work out your salvation. You are getting to be a fair pest in the house because of this temper. You are not to go and cuddle up this temper and say, 'I am a child of God, though I have a little infirmity.' Be saved from your infirmity, O sweet child of God! 'I do believe,' says another, 'I am in a state of grace, but I have a weakness for a dram.' Save yourself from that weakness, or, as Christmas is coming, you may be as drunk as any pagan! Another says, 'I do believe that I am saved, but I am inconsistent.' Well, save yourself from this inconsistency—work out your own salvation. What would you think of the man who went about with his hands in his pockets whistling and joking because he had a load of bricks and stones and timber lying all around there, and wanting shelter on a wintry day, he creeps under the bricks and says, 'This is my house: here will I dwell'? Are not some of us doing so? Why, if you could see your spiritual house as the Lord sees it, you would get in an awful fright. I grant the house has a foundation; if you are in Christ you are on the foundation, and, maybe,

there is a wee bit of the first course of masonry beginning
to rise, and a sort of indication of where the windows are
coming, and where the doors are to be, and there is just
a faint look as if there was a plan; but ye have stopped,
and though it is without a roof, and without walls, ye are
living as if the work were done. O man, work out your
own salvation!

"Up to-day, and at it. So we built the wall, says Nehe-
miah; with the sword in the one hand and the trowel
in the other, now working, now fighting, but never idle.
'Perfecting holiness, without which no man shall see the
Lord;' 'Looking diligently lest any man fail of the grace
of God;' 'Giving all diligence,' says Peter, 'add to your
faith virtue; and to virtue, knowledge; and to knowledge,
temperance; and to temperance, patience; and to patience,
godliness; and to godliness, brotherly kindness; and to
brotherly kindness, love itself.' That is the work to do.
First the foundation, and then all these rising tiers of
solid, graceful masonry. 'Work out your own salvation.'

"The next question is, How? Here is the *modus operandi*
—'with fear and trembling.' Do not make the mistake
that many are apt to make, who think this is a queer text
partly because it calls them to work, and partly because
it says 'with fear and trembling.' They have made it
a kind of gloomy ogre, and do not like to come near it.
It is like this dull, foggy time of the year, when we would
rather go to bed like the bears, and sleep through it, to
wake again in the spring. 'With fear and trembling'—
what does it mean? It does not mean that we are to go
through life with our knees forever smiting each other
because 'in such an hour as we think not' we will drop
into the pit again. Many take that meaning out of it,
and that paralyzes work. It does not mean a fear that
brings you into bondage, which brings the frost and chill

on your soul, that disjoins you from the almighty re-
sources of the Father's love and the Saviour's grace and
the Spirit's sanctifying power; but the fear rather which
makes you work sustainedly, eagerly, strenuously, unfail-
ingly.   It is a Bible expression, and it is only the Bible
which can expound it; it occurs in no other literature
under heaven except as a quotation from this old Book.
'Serve the Lord with fear, and rejoice with trembling,'
says the Scripture; 'Happy [not *miserable*] is the man
that feareth alway;' 'The fear of the Lord is the beginning of wisdom;' and so on.   Take a Bible concordance
and look down all the passages in which 'fear and trembling' is mentioned, and you will have an exposition of
Paul's words better than any I can give.

"It is like this: salvation is full; salvation is free; it is
a gift, and it is a gift from God without repentance.   He
will never change his mind.   'That is just where it will
spoil itself, preacher, don't you see?' says somebody.
'Men will take this salvation that is in Christ with eternal
glory, and then they will go away and live as they like.
What have you to say to this?'   Well, ever since the beginning the advocates of my gospel have just had to say
to that, '*It is not the fact.*'   It is those who take this salvation as the free gift of God who show the greatest hatred
of sin and greatest perseverance in striving against it.
We might misuse it so—it is a wonder of grace that we
do not, but we do not; and if any man here says, 'I will
take this eternal salvation and will go away and wallow
in sin'—you 'evil beast,' you will never get the chance,
never!   No soul thinks thus who has ever been made the
recipient of Divine Grace, none.   We may slip, we may
go back; but we will be ashamed of it, suffer for it, repent
of it, and return.

"'Work out your own salvation with fear and trembling.' The cup of salvation is so full, it is so brimming, it is so sweet, that it would be 'too sweet to be wholesome'; it *would* go to the head and make us reel and stagger, and become unwatchful and hilarious, and defeat its own purpose. But wherever Christ gives the cup of salvation he puts in an infusion of these tonic bitters, 'fear and trembling,' so that grace may not cloy and clog. These are the bitter herbs with which we eat our Passover. The more freely you take of Christ, the more careful you become in life and conduct; the more you look diligently, the more you walk circumspectly, looking where to put your foot next, for it is a dirty world, and the most careful may go over into the mud. 'Walk circumspectly, redeeming the time, because the days are evil.'

"It is like the ballast to the ship. You have seen a first-class yacht, a thing of beauty, and almost instinct with life. There it is; the sea is sparkling in the sun; there is a splendid, crisp breeze blowing. Watch that squall of wind as it strikes the yacht with its great mass and breadth of canvas that would do for the mainsail of a man-of-war. See what happens! You would expect the very breadth of the sheet is going to spoil all. That squall will strike the sail, and the vessel will careen and go to the bottom. Not at all: that squall strikes her, and most gracefully she yields to it and heels over on to her very beam end; but look at the cut-water. See how she is tearing through! For deep down there is the keel, and a great weight upon it; in these modern days tons of lead are run along the keel; or, as in your country, there is a great center-board sent away down into the water which gives tremendous leverage; and no matter how the yacht heels over, it holds her steady and prevents disaster. So with religion: spread your sails to the gales of gospel grace; take Christ in all the fulness of the Father's gift

as he is, and the gospel doctrines will not sink you; you
will not grow giddy and light-headed, but this fear and
trembling will give you rest, weight, grip, ballast, solidity,
and you will urge your course forward across these seas
of time and sin with splendid speed.

"It is just like what you have when a man has been
saved who was drowning, and all his kicking and struggling were only hastening it. And when this kicking and
struggling were over, some one has reached from above
and drawn him out, and there he stands on the solid
land, saved. Ah, but it was a narrow shave! Rejoicing,
but it is not a hilarious rejoicing, is it? He is not crack-
ing his thumbs and jigging, but he is rejoicing 'with
trembling.' He is altogether saved, and he was so nearly
altogether lost. Saved, blessed be God, saved!—cannot
some man shout hallelujah?—saved, but no thanks to us!
He sent from above and drew us and landed us on the
rock. We are saved, therefore we rejoice 'with fear and
trembling,' and after we have shaken the water off us,
we go steadily, calmly, circumspectly, never forgetting
that if it had not been for Grace we must have perished.

"'With fear and trembling.' Take another illustration.
An eminent French surgeon used to say to his students
when they were engaged in difficult and delicate opera-
tions, in which coolness and firmness were needed, 'Gentlemen, don't be in a hurry, for there's no time to lose.'
Time to make that incision once and well in the vital
place, not time to dash at it with over-confidence. Before
you have recovered yourself a precious life will have been
spilled.

"So, my believing brother and sister—I do not care what
your years may be—it is a word for all of us this evening.
Caution, diligence, a girding up of the loins, a wider opening of the eyes. 'Work out your own salvation with

fear and trembling'—no swagger, no bounce, no bravado, yet every confidence that He who hath begun this good work will carry it on to the perfect day. All confidence in Thee, my God, and none in myself; that is the way in which I do the best work toward God or my brother-man. Oh for sobriety to-day! How many converts begin and go on, and then—then comes a collapse. There are some here: you were converted, and with what splendid speed you began the Christian course—you did run well. What did hinder you? Ah! it is not the distance, but the pace that tells. You started off at too big a pace to keep it up; or, rather, you got away from your base of supplies, and you soon came to an end of yourself. It is just a few years since you began so well; and where are you to-day? You may be a Christian—you may be; but as regards activity, no one would know it. Your name is not found on the rolls of any Sabbath-school superintendents in Christendom: not one. You never come with tracts now; you never lift up a word of testimony for Christ now, and this is what spoiled you. Too confident, you began in the Spirit, and you went on in the flesh, and that which is born of the flesh is flesh, while that which is born of the Spirit is Spirit, and alone will endure and grow to all eternity. Come back, then, you who are nerveless and strengthless; you who are lying down in the middle of the course long before you have reached the end, come back to lowliness, to watchfulness, to self-distrust—'work out your own salvation with fear and trembling.' Only one life, no second chance forevermore; and into this one life, into this one day, we are to crowd, to pack the utmost of holy living in every direction that we possibly can, 'with fear and trembling.'

"I have left myself no time to deal with the thirteenth verse, 'For it is God that worketh in you;' but I just wish to recite it before I let you go. You work out, as one has said; for God works in. There is the mainspring, there is the unfailing Source, of all the believer's energy for sanctification, and for personal effort in the Church of Christ to promote his cause. It is God who worketh in us both to will and to do of his good pleasure. Then let me say at once, we can be holy, we *shall* be holy, for it is *God* who worketh in us. I will not stay even for a moment to discuss the question of sinless perfection. *That* is not your danger. Poor drunkard, thou canst give up drink; lustful man, thou canst be clean; for it is God, it is *God* that worketh in you. Do not be a football of the world, of the flesh, and the devil, for it is God that worketh in you. What tremendous emphasis we should bring to bear on that text! After all this calling on you to energy and to activity, I know that perhaps I depress you, for you said to yourself, 'Ah! it is true, it is all true; but what can I do?' Now we come back to the Power: 'It is God;' and what can he not do if you will only let him? God is the Source. See how he puts it. It is God that worketh in you. How? Listen: 'both to will and to do.' The first thing is to get the will right, and then the deed, don't you see, will follow. Is it not your complaint and mine that the will is wrong, the will is twisted, the will has been led captive by the devil? There are times when we can all enter into poor Augustine's complaint, 'Lord, I began to love thee too late: the devil was too long in me, the will got too much twisted, for although my heart goes after thee, my *will*—that is the mainspring, that is the rudder that turns the boat ofttimes as I do not want it to go.' God has gone down and down and down, deeper than the devil; God has bottomed thy will, and got down to the very spring of being; down at the spring and fount of thought and wish and imagination and effort,

CHAPTER XXXII.

SIXTEEN QUESTIONS ANSWERED.

AFTER the conclusion of his work in Chicago, the writer submitted to Mr. Moody a series of questions pertaining thereto, for the purpose of securing his own statements on certain points, to be used in this book, with the following result:

1. You have been in Chicago from the opening of the World's Fair to its close.. Do you think it has been, on the whole, a real benefit to the city, the country, and the world? Has it promoted the highest, truest interests of the people?

Answer. I think the Fair has been a great intellectual and material advantage to this land and to the world.

2. What, in your judgment, are the best results that have come from the Fair?

Answer. The best results that have come from the Fair are: first, the education it has afforded the common people; second, the broadening of our sympathies.

3. When and how did the thought and plan of this work suggest itself to you?

Answer. The plan of the World's Fair Gospel Campaign suggested itself about as soon as it was decided to bring the Fair to Chicago.

4. Have your plans been fully carried out, and your expectations realized?

229

Answer. My plans, as thought out before the opening of the campaign, have been enlarged and broadened as the work went on, and my highest expectations have been more than realized.

5. What are the principal results of the six months' work?

Answer. The principal result of our six months' work is, that millions have heard the simple gospel preached by some of the most gifted preachers in the world; thousands have apparently been genuinely converted to Christ, and Christians all over this land have been brought to a deeper spiritual life and aroused to more active Christian effort for the salvation of others; fires have been kindled in many parts of this land as a result of the summer campaign.

6. Have you learned any new lessons or suggestions about Christian work from your experience and observation during the six months' labors?

Answer. I have learned that the summer, so far from being the worst, is the best time to carry on Christian work in our cities. I have learned also to appreciate more than ever the power that there is in concentrated and united Christian action. I have been impressed with the fact that it is the Christian people of the land that take an interest in and patronize such expositions as the World's Fair.

7. Would such an extensive, long-continued series of gospel meetings be practicable and advisable at other times and places?

Answer. A gospel campaign carried out on extensive plans such as that in Chicago this summer I believe would be practicable and advisable in other large cities even where there was no fair.

8. Could such meetings be made a success without ex-

traordinary men as one of the attractions to draw the people?

Answer. In order that such meetings should be a success, the men most gifted in preaching the gospel that can be secured should be obtained.

9. After such extraordinary labors as yours, and after the visiting multitudes have left the city, do you think the churches should resume and continue their usual order and methods of work and service?

Answer. I believe that now, since the special effort is over and the visiting multitudes have left the city, the churches should continue their usual order and methods of work and service, only with more aggressiveness and increased effort.

10. Everybody will doubtless agree with you that great good has been done through your meetings, especially to the tens of thousands from afar who came hither; but will there not necessarily be a reaction after the crowds have gone and the extraordinary efforts have ceased?

Answer. So far as there being a reaction after the crowds have gone, I have reason to believe that there is increased spiritual life in many of the churches and a great outlook for the coming winter.

11. What do you consider to be the most effective agency, or agencies, in the prosecution of your campaign?

Answer. The most effective agencies in the prosecution of our campaign were the preaching and singing of the old gospel and the power of the Holy Ghost.

12. After the six months' experience of gospel meetings in connection with the Bible Institute, do you find any reason to change or modify the course of instruction or training there?

Answer. After this six months' experience I find no reason to essentially change or modify the course of instruction and training of the Bible Institute. I am more than ever convinced that we are on right lines, and that what is needed are men and women trained in the knowledge and practical use of the Word of God and in the use of their voices in gospel song.

13. What effect has the campaign had upon the Bible Institute?

Answer. As to the effect of the campaign on the Bible Institute, it has deepened the love for souls and earnestness in Christian effort of the students; has made them more than ever convinced that it is the preaching of the old gospel that draws men and lifts them up, and has given them the advantage of contact with the very best preachers in the world.

14. Will you gratify a curious public by stating what has been the aggregate expense of your entire six months' labors?

Answer. The entire expense of the six months' labor, exclusive of the ordinary expenses of the Institute, was $60,000, and $40,000 to enlarge the buildings before the time of the campaign.

15. Do you mind telling how those enormous expenses have been provided for?

Answer. These expenses were provided for by the gifts of generous Christian individuals and societies all over the United States, England, and Canada. Some of this money was given in answer to personal appeals, and some without any suggestion from me; but now that the campaign is over we are very close pressed for funds, as people have made an effort to help us through this special campaign.

16. What assurance, if any, did you have, at the beginning, that the means would be provided for the prosecution of the work?

Answer. The only assurance that I had in thinking that the necessary means for the work would be provided was that I knew the work ought to be done, and I knew that we had a God who would always sustain us in doing what we ought to do.

CHAPTER XXXIII.

THERE is no other participant with Mr. Moody in the work described in these pages who is more competent to give both a bird's-eye view of the whole grand movement and an interior view and just estimate of it, than Rev. R. A. Torrey, the superintendent of the Bible Institute. He was at the front and in the thick of the battle, and in the inner circle of its councils, from first to last, himself bearing with the commander-in-chief the burdens of its care and the responsibilities of leadership. On the occasion of the recent eighth session of the Christian Workers' Convention of the United States and Canada, in Atlanta, Ga., Mr. Torrey gave a masterly account of the movement, focused in one view, which will fitly serve as part of the conclusion of this fragmentary history of a work fully known only to the God of the harvest. Mr. Torrey spoke as follows:

"I am to speak to you upon the World's Fair City Evangelization Campaign. It was a great privilege to be associated with that campaign. I do not think that any of us who enjoyed that privilege will ever forget it. It is also a privilege to be able to tell you very briefly the story of that campaign, which, perhaps, stands alone in history as an organized attempt by the forces of Jesus Christ upon a great city in a time of great excitement.

"The campaign, as I presume most of you know, orig-

inated in the heart and brain of Mr. Moody. Mr. Moody
is so constituted by grace that he cannot see a great crowd
or hear of a great crowd without longing to preach the
gospel to them, and so when he heard of the vast crowds
that were gathered in Chicago from all parts of the world,
it seemed to him there was just one place in which to
spend the summer, and that was Chicago. He determined
to go there and preach the gospel of Jesus Christ, and
get all the noted preachers he could—or, rather, all the
preachers that God had peculiarly blessed in preaching
the Word of God—to go there with him. His idea was
that hitherto he had been going to the world, and that
now the world was coming to him. He thought he would
make one great attempt to reach the people from all parts
of the earth, as they should come to Chicago to see the
Fair, with the gospel of the Son of God. Very many
people thought the idea was visionary. They said that
people would come to Chicago to see the Fair, that they
would be there under large expense, that they would try
to get away as soon as possible, and therefore they would
spend all their time at the Fair seeing what they could
there. They pointed to the experience of past World's
Fairs. They said that Philadelphia, for example, at the
time of the Exposition, instead of being a place where
there was unusual spiritual interest, was a place where
there was unusual spiritual deadness and lack of interest.
They pointed also to the Exposition of Paris, and said the
same attempt had been made there and failed. There
seemed to be good ground for these forebodings. We
investigated the facts about the theaters, and we found
the leading opera troupes were fighting shy of Chicago;
and they showed their wisdom, for in point of fact when
they did open the theaters they had to shut them again,
because they could not get anybody to go to see the great-

est attractions in the theatrical line. Some ministers of excellent judgment said, 'Mr. Moody for once has made a mistake.' But we shall see that it was not a mistake. He thought he was led of God, and had faith that God would bless this attempt of his servant, and God did.

"Just a word about the forces that were rallied there in Chicago. First of all there was Mr. Moody himself, then John McNeill of London, who was with us the entire six months, except the first two weeks. Then there were with us noted men from England, and some of the best known men from this country. · Some of the men God blessed most came from the South—two men from Maryland, Mr. Dixon and Mr. Wharton, upon whose preaching God set his seal in a special way, and two from Texas, and one from North Carolina whom God singularly blessed. There were perhaps fifty noted preachers from different parts of the world; Dr. Pindor was there from Austria, Dr. Stoecker from Berlin, Rev. Theodore Monod from Paris, and others from other parts of Europe. We not only looked to preachers, but we looked to the singing of the gospel as well. Mr. Stebbins was with us almost the entire summer, Mr. Sankey, Mr. Towner, and many others of the best known gospel singers.

"After we got the forces there we did not know what we were going to do with them. We got the men before we laid our plans. We sent here and there and everywhere to famous preachers and singers, and invited them to come to Chicago. Then the question came, 'Now we have got our forces what are we going to do with them?'

"Let me sketch in outline the plan of campaign. First, we laid out three large sections. Chicago is naturally divided into three sections, by the river: the west side, the south side, and the north side. In each one of these sections we had a church center, these churches seating from 1800 to 2500 people each, and here we rallied our forces for meetings every night in the week and several services on Sunday. But we found these centers were not enough, and clustering around these centers we had to call many other churches into use. We did not stop at the churches. We next made an assault upon the theaters. Our faith was rather small at first, and we hired but one theater, the Haymarket, into which we could crowd 3500 people, and we did crowd it. The Haymarket Theater was not large enough, so we rented the Empire Theater across the way and filled that, and then we had to get the Standard Theater, three blocks away, but that was not enough. Then we got the Columbia Theater, and then we engaged Music Hall and held services there every day for two hours, from eleven to one o'clock, and three services on Sunday. But that was not enough, so we engaged Hooley Opera House. That was not enough, so we engaged the Grand Opera House, and on several other Sundays other theaters; so we had going every Sunday six theaters in addition to these churches. But we found a great number of people living and staying about the Fair grounds, and our next question was to get buildings about the Fair; so we got the Model Sunday-school Building, the Epworth Hotel and the Christian Endeavor Tabernacle, and, toward the end of the season, a theater seating 1800. That was not enough, and so we put up temporary buildings. We had five tents in different parts of the city. One of the tents was small, seating about 400. Three of them seated 1000 each, and the fifth tent seated 1500 people. We thought we had a big enough tent then, but we found a seating capacity of 1500 was not enough; so we put seats outside the tent for 500 people more and threw up the curtains and had 2000 people every night after that. But we found that was not enough, so we sent on to Mr. Collins, or rather he sent on to us, the gospel carriage that is owned by the Bureau of Supplies, and we went about in that to different parts of the city holding meetings; but that was not enough, so we went out into the open air and held meetings in different parts of the city. That was not enough, and so we had cottage meetings; and that was not enough, so we went to the jails and hospitals and police stations and preached the gospel in the jails to about 600, and in the police stations to the policemen, to those in hospitals and other institutions.

"Now we thought as long as the whole world was coming to Chicago we ought to try to reach all nations, and so we sent over to Germany for Dr. Stoecker, the famous preacher—perhaps the most famous in the world—to come over and preach to the Germans. There was a great deal of opposition to his coming on the part of some, for they said people would not come out to hear him. The first Sunday he was there Music Hall was packed to suffocation and hundreds were sent away. We got a preacher for the Swedes, who preached to 1500 of them nightly. We sent to Paris for a preacher to preach to the French, and one of our own students preached to the Bohemians. And so we reached all these different nations by the preaching of the gospel. There was one other source of strength, and that was the students of the Institute. Perhaps I ought to say that all this work was conducted under the leadership and in the name of the Bible Institute. There we had a hundred and fifty men at our command and seventy women. Some of them preached, some of them sang, some of them helped in the inquiry meeting, and all of them were willing to help in almost any way they could. Mr. Moody said: 'This campaign could never have been carried on except for the Bible Institute. If there was any part of the city where we needed to throw a detachment, we had them at our command. If we only had a few hours' notice we could send fifty men over to that part of the city and placard and ticket the whole neighborhood and fill a building.' So much for the outline of the work.

"Now we come to the interest that the work awakened. And let me say right here that the interest was far beyond the expectation of any of us. One thing will illustrate the interest, and that was the crowds that attended the services. We had a great many services, I cannot tell you how many services, every night, and a hundred and ten to a hundred and fifteen every Sunday. The audiences on the closing Sundays of the campaign were from 70,000 to 75,000 per Sunday—rather a large number of persons. Take, for example, the Haymarket Theater, where the service was announced to begin at half-past ten, and I presume there are people in this building who got there at five minutes past ten and you did not get in. Fifteen minutes before ten o'clock the street in front would be blocked, and when the door was opened the building, which by excessive packing would accommodate 3500 people, would be filled in five minutes. Then we would tell them to go three blocks below to the Standard Theater. One Sunday, after 3500 people were in the Haymarket and 2300 in the Standard, there were 1000 turned away to find accommodations where they could. Go to Music Hall in the afternoon and you would find that full. Go to Immanuel Church on Michigan Avenue for the three-o'clock service and you would find that full, and every night at seven o'clock you would find the church packed to suffocation with from 2200 to 2500 people; and go three blocks away to the Plymouth Church and you would find that full and people turned away. I never

saw such hunger to hear the Word of God in my life.
People would come at ten o'clock and stay until twelve
o'clock. When Mr. Moody was through preaching he
would say, 'Now I have a friend I want you to hear,'
while I stood there in fear and trembling. I was afraid
that everybody would go. We stood up to sing a hymn,
and he said that any who wanted to go could do so, but
nearly everybody stayed to hear the next speaker. That
sort of thing went on week after week. Toward the end
of the campaign we held three all-day meetings in Music
Hall. We began at half-past nine in the morning and
closed at half-past three in the afternoon. The people
were there as soon as the doors opened, and at two of
those meetings I watched the audience, and I believe there
were over a thousand people who stayed right through
without a mouthful to eat, from half-past nine in the morning to half-past three in the afternoon; and I have a sus-
picion if we had gone on to six or half-past they would
have stayed there still. Perhaps the best illustration of
the interest in the meetings was 'Chicago Day.' As you
know, Chicago Day was the great day of the Fair, and
everybody went to the Fair on Chicago Day, or they were
expected to. Over 700,000 people, in point of fact, did
pass through the gates of the Fair. The question came
up as to whether we would try to hold a meeting on Chicago Day, and it was decided that we would, and that
right in the very heat of the day, from ten o'clock till
half-past two. We went down to Music Hall wondering
whether any one would come or not, and we found the
hall packed full and people turned away. At one of
our all-day meetings where I was to preside, and where I
thought it would be easy to get in, they came near losing
their presiding officer, for I could not get in myself till I
found a back door and got to my seat upon the platform.

"Another thing that showed the interest in the Word of God was the fact that people from different places staying only a few days at the Fair, having perhaps only one opportunity to see the fireworks, would turn their backs upon some of the best pyrotechnic displays ever produced, and go to the Model Sunday-school Building or into the Epworth Hotel. While the rockets and while the different kinds of fireworks were bursting in the air, they turned their backs upon the whole scene and went into those places to hear the Word of God. Women would go elegantly dressed to those meetings and find every seat taken; but they would be so interested they would sit down on the bare floor of the tent in order to get an opportunity to listen. One night there was a great storm of rain, and it blew in under the sides of the tent, and the water stood in puddles on the floor of the tent, and the question was, should there be a meeting; but there was a unanimous vote for the meeting, and there they sat, with the rain coming down through the roof and blowing in under the sides, and gathering in pools on the floor, so hungry were they to hear the Word of God. The question has often been asked, Where do these people that attend the meetings come from? One of the Chicago papers, or rather one of the reporters, said to Mr. Moody one day, 'You are not reaching World's Fair people. These are all Chicago people.' So we got into the habit of putting it to vote to find out how many were World's Fair people, and time and time again, when we made a test, seven eighths, nine tenths, and sometimes nineteen twentieths of the audience would stand up, testifying they were not Chicago people but from the four quarters of the earth. A great many people who came up to the World's Fair dropped into our meetings and went to our meetings more than they did to the Fair. I think a good many people came to Chicago to go to the Fair who never went there at all. I remember one gentleman, to whom I was talking one day, said, 'I came to take in the World's Fair, but I have not been to the World's Fair. I have been at your lectures here every morning, and I go to your meetings every night.'

"Some one will say, 'What was the result of this work, and did it pay for the large expenditure of money?' It did cost money. It cost a good many thousand dollars. What were the results of the work? The first result was that thousands and hundreds of thousands of people heard the gospel in its simplicity and power, many who had never heard it before. I was trying to figure it up as I came down to-night, and as near as I can get at it two million people, not different people, but two million people heard the gospel in our various services this summer, and quite likely more than that. The next thing in the way of results was conversions. You ask me, How many conversions? I cannot tell you. I do not believe in counting conversions anyhow, but this I do know, that there were scores in single meetings that gave evidence of having accepted Jesus Christ as their Saviour. Let me give a single illustration of the last meeting in Haymarket Theater. At the close of that service everybody who had determined that morning to accept Christ was invited to come up and shake hands with me, and receive a little book on the Christian life; and there I stood in front of the platform, I know not how long, and a great line of young men, old men, young women, and middle-aged women came up one after another, and I put to them the question, 'Have you decided to take Jesus Christ as your personal Saviour and confess him before the world from this time?' and that great, long line of men and women, young and old, came up and said, 'Yes.' That same night, in Immanuel Baptist Church, in the south part of the

city, I stood in front of the pulpit with the same question,
and man after man and woman after woman came up and
said they had accepted the Lord Jesus Christ that night.

"Another of the marked characteristics of the work was
the number of young men reached. A very large proportion of the audiences were young men, and a very large
proportion of those who accepted Christ were young men.
For example, in a single meeting—it was a very notable
meeting—a hundred and eighteen young men stood up
to say definitely and clearly that that afternoon they had
taken the Lord Jesus Christ as their personal Saviour.
Now these men came from all classes of society, and some
of the converts were of a very notable character. For
example, our meetings in the Empire Theater and Standard Theater were different from most of the others. They
were practically slum meetings. In one of these meetings
there sat a civilized Indian who was engaged as an engineer, but he had never heard the gospel. As he sat
there and heard of the love of God he trusted in Jesus
Christ as his Saviour. The moment he accepted Christ
his heart went out to his fellow-Indians. He came to my
brother and said, 'Are you a preacher?' 'I preach sometimes.' 'I have got a lot of Indians down here. They
are medicine-men living down here in an alley, and I want
you to come down and preach to them.' And he took my
brother away down to that alley where those Indian medicine-men were gathered, and he preached the gospel to
them. He said it was the most attentive audience he ever
had. He took my brother to his home and pointed to his
little boy, five years old, and said: 'Do you see that boy?
Well, I heard your brother preach about the love of God,
and I have accepted Jesus Christ as my Saviour. I had
never heard about the love of God before. I have consecrated that boy to Jesus Christ, and I am going to bring

him up to preach the gospel and send him to preach to
the Indians.'

"Quite a large number of actors were converted in the
meetings. I want to say we not only used these regular
places for meetings, but when anything extraordinary
came along we used that. For example, Forepaugh's circus
spent two Sundays in Chicago, and we engaged their tent,
which accommodated 15000 people. Those who could not
find seats stood up in the arena, and it was estimated that
15000 or 20000 people came to the circus to hear about
the love of God in Jesus Christ. It was a terribly hot
day, and it seemed as if we would all die before the service
was over; but there that great crowd of men and women
sat and stood beneath the overheated canvas, the perspira-
tion rolling down their faces, and listened to the gospel.
Among those brought to Christ on that morning was an
actor, a man who had made a wreck of his life through
strong drink. A large number of men and their wives
were brought to Christ. Some people from the very highest classes of society were converted. For example, among
the young men converted is one of whom I will tell you.
A certain business man who has business interests in
Chicago, who gives us thousands of dollars every year for
our work, and has given us several thousand dollars this
year, had an unconverted son. He was deeply interested
in him. This boy came to Chicago and came to our meetings in Haymarket Theater. One night at the close of the
service he walked up on to the stage, took Mr. Moody by
the hand, and told him he had accepted Jesus Christ as
his Saviour. That father thinks he has invested his thousands well.

"The best part of the results, however, was not the
conversions. You may be surprised at the statement, but
I think it is true that the best part of the work was not

the conversions, although I suppose if we were to number them there would be thousands who accepted Jesus Christ as their Saviour this summer in our meetings. The best part of the work was the arousing and instructing of Christians. Christians came to Chicago from all over the world. They came to our meetings, and many of them received the baptism of the Holy Ghost. Many others were stimulated to Christian work. They have gone back to their homes. In various parts of this country, North, South, East, and West, little fires of revival interest have been kindled because of what these people heard in Chicago. I do not know, but I presume there are many here to-night who could stand up and testify that some one went from their community to Chicago and came back on fire, and interest has been awakened in their community. Hundreds of ministers were stirred up to new devotion and new power in the service of Jesus Christ.

"On one of the closing Sunday mornings of the campaign, when the Haymarket Theater overflowed, and the overflow meeting had filled the Standard Theater, where I had gone to preach, I looked over the audience, and it seemed to me that the whole audience was largely composed of Christians, and I put to them the question, 'How many of you are strangers in Chicago?' There were 2500 people in the theater, all we could pack in, and we had to turn several hundred away that morning. That whole audience rose. I could not see ten people in that whole audience that did not rise to their feet. As I looked into their faces I became very confident they were not only strangers but Christian people, and I saw a great many ministers of the gospel; so, looking up to God for guidance, I chose the baptism of the Spirit of God as the subject to speak upon. At the close of the service a fine-looking gentleman came to me on the platform and said:

'Sir, I have not this baptism you have been talking about. I am a minister of the gospel, a Presbyterian minister. I have had fruit in my ministry, but I do not believe I have received the baptism of the Holy Ghost. I want you to pray for me that I may receive it.' 'Why not here and now?' I said. He hesitated a moment and then said, 'I will.' We turned around and knelt by the chair, and another gentleman came up and said, 'Can I kneel with you?' I said, 'Certainly.' We knelt in prayer. I prayed, and this Presbyterian minister prayed, and the other gentleman prayed. When we arose to our feet I turned to the other gentleman and said: 'Are you a minister?' 'No, I am a judge; but, friends, I am a Christian and a Sunday-school superintendent, and I need the baptism of the Spirit of God as much as a minister does.' Now this thing happened: ministers and laymen, young men and young women from societies of Christian Endeavor all over this country, came up to Chicago, heard the possibility of a higher phase of Christian life presented, and I believe this winter all over the United States of America we are going to see an evangelistic interest kindled through the work done in Chicago this summer.

"One thing more I wish to say before I sit down. We learned four lessons this summer. Four things were demonstrated. The first was that the summer is a good time to do aggressive Christian work. You believe that already in the South, but it is not believed in the North. The view in the North is that the time to do active work is in January, right after the Week of Prayer, and perhaps keep it up till May, certainly not later than June, and then let up till the fall comes around. We demonstrated in Chicago this summer that the summer was the very best time to reach men with the gospel of the Son of God.

"Another thing that we demonstrated was—it needed

no demonstration, however—that the old gospel had lost nothing of its power. You hear it oftentimes said to-day that you have got to get up some new doctrine, some new views of truth, to reach men and hold them. You notice these men that get up new views and new doctrines don't hold the people very long; but the old gospel does hold them. The only thing preached in our churches or theaters or tents was the simple doctrine of the atoning blood of the Son of God and the power of the gospel to save perishing men, and people came by the thousands, came by the ten thousands—until we had to turn them away— just to hear the old story of the cross and the power of Jesus Christ to save. I do not know that it is quite fair to tell it here, but I think you will permit it. A man came to Chicago this summer with the idea that a new theology would draw great crowds. He had been invited to speak at one of our congresses, one of our religious congresses. He was completely infatuated with his new theology views, and he wrote a paper. It was the effort of his life. Then he passed it around to his friends for criticism. Then he re-shaped it and sent it around again. He re-wrote that paper four times. Then he thought he had it perfect, and came to Chicago to read it. He had visions of Columbus Hall with a great throng of thousands of people gathered to listen to this great effort of his life. The hour to deliver that paper came, and with trembling and with expectation he went into the hall and looked over his audience, and he had sixteen women and two men to hear his paper. But, friends, the old gospel did not have to look out on an audience of sixteen women and two men; but oftentimes on an audience of thousands of men alone, 3500 one time, 7000 another time, 15000 another time, gathered in one place to listen to the old gospel as we find it in the Word of God.

"Another thing we demonstrated this summer is that
all you have to do to reach the masses is what President
Candler told you this afternoon, 'Go and reach them.'

"The fourth and last thing we demonstrated—and that
don't need any demonstration—is the power of prayer.
If you were to ask me to-night what I thought was the
great secret of this marvelous success, I would say it was
this : that the leaders in this movement looked up to God
to give the victory and expected him to do it and he did
it. We were disappointed in men. Some of the men
whom we expected the most of we got the least out of,
and some of the men we expected least out of we got the
most out of. But we were never disappointed in God. He
helped us all along the line. He helped us in getting the
blessing in the meetings, he helped us in overcoming obstacles, and he helped us in getting the money we needed.
I do not know how many thousands of dollars it cost.
We are figuring that up now. I presume they know now,
but they did not know when I left Chicago; but, friends,
it was in answer to prayer that money came. I do not
mean that people were not asked to give, because they
were asked to give all over this country, and they did
give most generously; but time and time again we got
into a corner and there was no man to go to, and we went
to God, who brought us out of our difficulty. Let me
give you a single illustration of that. It was in August.
Mr. Moody had to go East. It was near the 10th of the
month. We pay part of our bills on the 1st of the month
and part on the 10th. Four thousand dollars had to be
paid on the 10th of that month. Mr. Moody was to go
away in a day or two, and there was no money to pay it.
We did not know what to do. Mr. Moody gathered some
of us together, the inner circle of workers, at the dinner-
table in his room. A great burden was upon his heart.

He did not know where the money was to come from. I
do not think he was discouraged; but I think he was as
near discouraged as I ever saw him in my life. We sat
down to that table. Just before we were seated a letter
came inclosing an English letter of credit for nearly a
thousand dollars. There was a prayer going up from the
heart of Mr. Moody and from the hearts of two or three
others who knew of the dilemma we were in. As we sat
at that dinner-table a man came in with a telegram. He
took it to Mr. Moody. Mr. Moody opened the telegram
and then passed it down to me. That telegram read:
'Your friends at Northfield have given to-day as a free-
will offering six thousand dollars for your work in Chicago, and there is more to follow.' Four thousand dollars
more did follow, ten thousand in all. Friends, need I tell
you we did not finish that meal? We pushed back with
one accord from the table, and knelt by our chairs, and
with tears and sobs lifted our hearts in gratitude to God.
He had heard our cry, and while we were yet speaking
had answered our prayer. And so it was all this summer.
Men often failed us, difficulties often came, but we had
one Friend that always stood by us, and when money ran
short, when the meetings grew dull, when obstacles came
up and doors seemed closed, we went alone with God and
we looked up to God for his blessing and for his power,
and God heard us every time. The money came and the
obstacles went, and, best of all, the Spirit of God came
down."

CHAPTER XXXIV.

CONCLUDING ESTIMATES.

IT is not too much to say that the World's Fair Gospel Campaign marks an epoch in Christian evangelism. It was a distinct, new departure, a "forward movement" on a new track. Out of it will doubtless grow results as far-reaching as anything that Mr. Moody has ever done. There is no doubt that, as one result of the lessons there learned, evangelistic work will be organized with different methods and on a larger scale than ever before. Some hoary old fallacies about the impossibility of maintaining religious services in summer and about the unattractiveness of gospel meetings forever lost their grip in Chicago during those days. It is true, as Mr. Moody says, that there is nothing more attractive than the gospel of Jesus Christ, presented in sermon and song, with the power of the Holy Spirit.

The Boston *Congregationalist* says: "Mr. Moody's six months' campaign in Chicago has been a marvelous success, greater than even he had anticipated. Looked at from the human side alone, it has not been any less wonderful than the Fair itself and its allied congresses. If the display in Jackson Park appealed to the eye and the æsthetic sense, the congresses in the Art Palace to the intellect and the love of knowledge, Mr. Moody's meetings have appealed to the religious sense. Hundreds of thousands from every section of the country and from all over the world have heard the gospel from the lips of the great evangelist or from some one of his helpers.

"During this entire period the interest has increased rather than diminished. From Mr. Moody himself it has been the same old story, almost in the very words which he has used for a score of years, but it has lost none of its freshness, none of its influence on the multitude. What a testimony to the power of the gospel were those all-day meetings in Central Music Hall, where hundreds were unable to secure entrance! All summer the tents used in certain sections of the city have been crowded. The meetings in theaters, too, have been very popular. Even the owners of these theaters are said to have been favorably disposed toward Mr. Moody and inclined to aid him in his work. But the churches have not been empty when Mr. Moody or any of his helpers were announced to speak. Nor, in general, has there been any lack of attendants when the regular pastors have spoken.

"The summer campaign in Chicago has shown that people are not weary of the gospel, that when preachers present it with earnestness they are not unwilling to go into the churches to hear it. It has proved, also, that no men are more thoroughly in sympathy with the people, or more anxious to do them good, or more eager to bring them the gospel as it is found in the New Testament, than the pastors of the various evangelical churches in our cities. Without the aid of these pastors Mr. Moody's success would have been far less than it has proved to be."

The editor of the *Epworth Herald*, in a review of the work, says: "The evangelistic campaign carried on during the whole period of the Fair under Mr. Moody's direction did not attract as much attention as its importance and usefulness deserved. Nevertheless it accomplished a vast amount of good. Mr. Moody did not plan a series of re-

vival services. While soul-winning was kept in view, the
primary design of the meetings was to arrest the attention
of the tens of thousands who thronged here, and compel
the people to think upon religious things. The inspiration and authority of the Scriptures, the follies of infidelity, the danger of worldliness, human responsibility,
personal accountability, the certainty of punishment, and
kindred themes, were emphasized in no uncertain terms.
Calls to slumbering Christians and careless sinners were
full of tenderness, eagerness, and warmth.

"Concerning the practical results of the campaign it is
difficult to speak with exactness. The congregations were
gathered from all parts of the world. They were constantly changing. Many persons heard the evangelists
only once. The fruitage of labor put forth under such
circumstances cannot be gathered right away. But *some-
where* and at *some time* the harvest will appear. No figures
can represent the impression left upon thousands of persons who, but for these extraordinary meetings (the ordinary services at the churches were crowded), might not
have heard the gospel warning and the gospel call. The
chief aim of the campaign, as I have said, was not revival-
istic. The effort was to preach and sing the gospel to the
surging thousands, and neutralize, to the greatest possible
extent, the bad influences which beset World's Fair visitors. In reaching this result the effort seems to have been
signally successful. This Moody campaign will undoubt-
edly go into history as one of the most sagacious and influential religious movements of this century."

The editor of the *Ram's Horn*, who had every facility
for studying and participating in the movement, says:
"Never in the history of the world was such a time known
in religious annals as that through which Chicago passed
during the World's Columbian Exposition season. While

we have watched the World's Parliament of Religions with
wonder, we felt as we might if witnessing some grand review of marshaled hosts; but when with intenser interest
we turned to see this most remarkable battle for truth
and right and the coming of the kingdom of Christ in our
midst, it seemed as though we were watching the militant
hosts of Immanuel moving into action and striking the
very strongholds of satanic power, not only in Chicago,
but the whole world over. As far as our farthest guests
shall go to their distant homes will the influences of this
wonderful work follow and be felt forever. . . .

"From the farthest suburbs to the very center of civic
life, in the most beautiful quarters, along magnificent
boulevards, to the lowest slums of our city, the effect of
this movement has been felt. But Chicago is not the only
place to be benefited by this wonderful work. The hundreds of thousands which thronged these great gatherings
came from every land on earth. Every State in the great
Republic sent a host of representatives. Returning to
their homes over the whole wide world, they have taken
with them the influences of the lessons to which they have
listened, the songs they have heard, and the enthusiasm
here inspired.

"To sum up the results of such a work is impossible
for man. It cannot be measured in time, for eternity
alone can tell, and God alone knows, how many hundreds
of thousands of hearts have been and will be reached."

The *Union Signal* begins an editorial review of the work
of the six months with the following words: "Among the
many and diverse movements more or less directly connected with the Fair, there was one unique in its conception, unparalleled in its success, world-wide in its influence,
and yet one concerning which the newspapers had com-
paratively little to say, and whose magnitude and signifi-

cance is perhaps the least appreciated of any of the adjuncts
of the exposition. It is the movement which Mr. Torrey
aptly calls the 'World's Fair City Evangelization Campaign.' By the side of this great, victorious, peaceful
campaign of faith for the redemption of the world, the
bloody campaigns of the Napoleons of earth pale into in-
significance."

The article concludes with these words: "If any have
mourned 'as those without hope' over the Sunday opening of the Fair, the triumph of the liquor traffic in the
White City, if they have supposed that sin held undis-
puted sway in the World's Fair city, and only demoraliza-
tion has attended the great Exposition, let him take courage. We believe that the 'World's Fair City Evangelization Campaign' wrought more effectively for the kingdom
of God than all the combined forces of evil were able to
accomplish against it."

It need hardly be said that it is impossible to tabulate
the good results of a work such as has been so imperfectly
described. Figures and records fail to embrace the whole
fact. It must suffice to say here that multitudes of all
classes and conditions of the unconverted, as well as professed Christians, were savingly affected by the gospel
preached and sung. Conversions were a daily occurrence,
sometimes numbering scores in a single service, especially
in the theaters and the tents, where some of the lowest
and the vilest from the city slums were gloriously saved,
as well as many a wild, reckless visitor from afar, while
without doubt many thousands of Christians were renewed, instructed, strengthened, and inspired for better
life and service.

In any attempt to estimate results the remarkable fact
must be kept in mind that of the hundreds of thousands
who thronged the meeting-places, an immense majority

were World's Fair visitors from all parts of this and other lands, and that the congregations were daily changing and daily new. It is not in Chicago, therefore, that the fruits of the six months' labor must be sought; but in every State in the Union, and in other lands, wherever the millions who streamed in and out of Chicago during the Fair have gone back to their homes and churches, there the greatest results may be expected to become manifest as the days go by.

Another remarkable fact to be noted in such an estimate is the large number of preachers, students, and Christian workers of all kinds who were in attendance upon the meetings; as, for example, at the Fair grounds, where not less than one thousand preachers were present during the meetings of a single week, and in Central Music Hall from one hundred to two hundred at a single service, while in all the principal meetings the ministers constituted an important part of the congregations. These facts alone warrant the confident expectation of far-reaching results of revival and renewal in churches and homes throughout the land whither these people, with their renewed love and zeal, have gone.

www.ingramcontent.com/pod-product-compliance
Lightning Source LLC
Chambersburg PA
CBHW020850270326
41928CB00006B/631